CASA
MODERNA

CASA MODERNA
LATIN AMERICAN LIVING

PHILIP JODIDIO

WITH OVER 250 ILLUSTRATIONS

CONTENTS

MY HOUSE IS MY REFUGE

CONTEMPORARY LATIN AMERICAN HOUSES

In 2015, the Museum of Modern Art in New York organized an exhibit titled "Latin America in Construction: Architecture 1955-1980." The curator, Barry Bergdoll, commented, "I was stunned by how Latin America had been systematically not part of my own historical education in architecture—despite the fact that I have three degrees in art and architectural history. Most history books on modern architecture in the English language assign a subordinate role to Latin America..." Today, information about contemporary architecture circulates more freely over the internet, and the role played by Latin American architects has been increasingly recognized. While the great Brazilian architect Oscar Niemeyer (1907-2012) had to share his 1988 Pritzker Prize with the American Gordon Bunshaft (1909-90), the Chilean Alejandro Aravena (1967-), the sole 2016 winner, was judged by the Pritzker jury to be "leading a new generation of architects that has a holistic understanding of the built environment." They went on to say that Aravena "clearly demonstrate[s] the ability to connect social responsibility, economic demands, design of human habitat and the city. Few have risen to the demands of practicing architecture as an artful endeavor, as well as meeting today's social and economic challenges. Aravena, from his native Chile, has achieved both, and in doing so has meaningfully expanded the role of the architect." In fact, Aravena was that year curating the Venice Architecture Biennale, a sure sign that Latin American architecture is today in the mainstream of international creativity. Two years earlier, in 2014, another Chilean architect, Smiljan Radic, designed the Serpentine Pavilion in London. These innovative architects, rising to international status from a country with just 18.3 million inhabitants—compared with the United States' 326 million—are surely an indication that there is new creativity in Latin America, and of a different sort from the early Modernism that sprang up on the continent in the 1930s.

As in other parts of the world, residential architecture offers Latin American architects some of their most significant opportunities to explore their craft and to express their originality. Private clients, often with considerable means, seek perhaps to indulge themselves, but in the process allow the design of structures that could otherwise only exist in architects' imaginations. It would be inappropriate to identify any dominant style in contemporary Latin American houses, but they do seem to share a particular spirit; the often favorable climate encourages a thorough interpenetration of interior and exterior, with many houses having generous terraces and ingenious openings that can double their usable area in good weather. Some are even designed with a bias toward the outdoors, albeit with spaces that may be covered to protect from rain or sun.

JUNGLE GROWTH IN THE WORST SENSE...

"I saw some shocking things," wrote the Swiss architect and designer Max Bill in his "Report from Brazil," published in the October 1954 issue of the *Architectural Review*: "Modern architecture sunk to the depth, a riot of anti-social waste, lacking any sense of responsibility towards either the business occupant or (its) customers.... Here is utter anarchy in a building, jungle growth in the worst sense..." The structure that so challenged his sensibilities was Oscar Niemeyer's California Building in São Paulo, built in 1955. This curious meeting of Swiss rigor and Brazilian Modernism may indeed mark a turning point in the development of Latin American architecture. Bergdoll, reflecting on the Museum of Modern Art's 2015 exhibition, stated, "Our hypothesis was that these criticisms led to Latin American architects adopting stronger theoretic positions on what their architecture was about. So what we're looking at is the aftermath of this critique. The euphoric period has ended, and architecture becomes both more eclectic and emphatically engaged." The MoMA exhibition looked at the period between 1955 and 1980, but even in the more recent houses published in this volume, Bergdoll's observation of a less euphoric and more eclectic spirit still seems to hold true.

ONE CONTINENT, TWENTY COUNTRIES

Quite obviously, Latin America is not in any sense to be considered as a single entity, in terms of aesthetics, economics, or even language. Brazil, with its population of over 200 million, has a distinct history that differentiates it from the rest of the continent. Brazil is the country of Niemeyer, but also of more recent major architects such as the Modernist Lina Bo Bardi (1914-92) and Paulo Mendes da Rocha (1928-), winner of the 2006 Pritzker Prize. To the north, Mexico, with its long-standing ties to the United States (recent political events notwithstanding) and population of over 125 million, has a powerful architectural tradition marked by such figures as Luis Barragán (1902-88), winner

of the 1980 Pritzker Prize, or Pedro Ramírez Vázquez (1919–2013), creator of Mexico City's National Museum of Anthropology. With a design that surely sought to tie his modern vision to that of Mexico's ancient history, Ramírez Vázquez encountered the disapproval of the Mexican poet Octavio Paz, who stated in 1969 that the "exaltation and glorification of Mexico-Tenochtitlan transforms the Museum of Anthropology into a temple." The next most populous of the twenty countries of Latin America are Colombia (48 million) and Argentina (nearly 44 million). As the success of Chilean architects demonstrates, however, the architectural inventiveness of Latin America is not strictly limited to the larger nations. The architectural traditions of these countries, and others of the continent, have been shaped by their economic or political difficulties. The continent has, for many years, registered comparatively slow economic growth, high poverty, inequality, poor levels of education and slow technological progress. There are significant barriers between different segments of the population, more and less advantaged groups, indigenous (or black) and "white," highly educated and poorly educated.[1] Of course, the proportions of each of these elements are different in each country, but architecture clearly emerges more readily from areas that do not suffer from systemic sources of instability.

I LEFT TO CREATE LIGHTER THINGS

Fundamental to the contemporary architecture of Latin America is its relation to the creativity that has flowed from other parts of the world, and in particular Europe. It is often assumed that the colonial influence of "the West" was the dominant force; Oscar Niemeyer famously worked under Lúcio Costa with Le Corbusier on the design of the Ministry of Education in Rio in 1936, marking the arrival of European-derived Modernism in the official architecture of Brazil. But of this encounter and its subsequent impact, there have been differing accounts. "I was on the path of Le Corbusier," Niemeyer himself said in 2004, "but I left it to create lighter things." Ultimately, it may well have been Niemeyer who had an impact on Le Corbusier. In his autobiography Niemeyer declares, "It was obvious that my architecture had influenced Le Corbusier's later projects, but this factor is only now being taken into account by critics of his work." He goes on to cite the memoirs of

Amédée Ozenfant, the painter with whom Le Corbusier set out the doctrines of Purism in the book Après le cubisme (1918). "After so many years of purist discipline and loyalty to the right angle," Ozenfant writes, "Le Corbusier caught wind of the premise of a new baroque from elsewhere, and he seems to have decided to leave aside the honest right-angle, which he tended to regard as his private domain for so long." The impact of Niemeyer and other Latin Americans—like Luis Barragán, who certainly influenced Tadao Ando (minus the color)—on the rest of the world is clear today. It is obvious that the architecture of Latin America is on a par with that of any other region; inventive, often powerful and unexpected, as many of the houses published here demonstrate.

INSIDE-OUT

Looking to Japan while approaching Latin American homes might be unexpected, but some of the core ideas of Modernism, particularly in residential architecture, can be traced to the German Bruno Taut (1880–1938) and his travels in the Far East. He arrived in Japan in 1933 at the invitation of the Japanese Association for International Architecture. In 1935, Taut claimed to be the "discoverer" of Katsura, referring to the Katsura Imperial Villa, built in Kyoto in the 17th century. He was fascinated by Katsura's "modernity," and this fascination was inherited by Le Corbusier and Walter Gropius (1883–1969). These architects saw in its undecorated orthogonal and modular spaces parallels to contemporary Modernism, even going so far as to identify Katsura as a "historical" example of modernity. The Modernists saw what they wanted to see in Katsura— a Mondrian-like simplicity—while ignoring its rustic side, as well as the "complexity and contradiction" that lies in almost every aspect of the buildings and gardens. Though the weather in Japan is not usually as clement as that of much of Latin America, the ambiguity between interior and exterior expressed in shoji (sliding screens) and the engawa (a passageway or veranda that is neither fully inside nor fully outside the main structure), are inscribed in the DNA of many of the contemporary houses published here. The leading architects of 20th-century Latin America may not cite traditional Japanese architecture as their influence, but it was undoubtedly a presence in the founding of Modernism, which unquestionably underlies much of the contemporary architecture of this "new" continent. The frequent use of sliding screens to frame specific views, seen often in Japan, is mirrored here in sliding windows that open interiors toward spectacular views of the continent's coasts and mountains. Indeed, a fundamental ambiguity between inside and out unites these contemporary designs.

AT THE OCEAN'S EDGE

There is a conscious decision on the part of contemporary architects to insert these houses into their natural setting, combining modern comfort with an awareness of place that is often extreme; houses hover above the ocean or disappear into dense forest. Elevations frequently show a direct relation to topography; site plans that include topographical lines make it possible to visualize the intent of the architect given the nature of the location. A glance at the plans of the houses published here (see pp. 306–12) quickly confirms that rectilinear designs of varying complexity are the rule, with the curves of which Niemeyer was so fond all but absent. Local stone, brick and wood, with an increasing awareness of ecological issues, are combined with the materials typical of the contemporary worldwide palette, favoring concrete, steel and glass. Local foliage tends to be retained here, more so than in other parts of the world.

AN EMOTIONAL PIECE OF ARCHITECTURE

"My house is my refuge," Luis Barragán once wrote; "an emotional piece of architecture, not a cold piece of convenience." Though formally quite rectilinear and strict, Barragán's houses can be seen as a rebuttal to Le Corbusier's diktat that "a house is a machine for living in." Barragán further stated, "It is alarming that publications devoted to architecture have banished from their pages the words Beauty, Inspiration, Magic, Spellbound, Enchantment, as well as the concepts of Serenity, Silence, Intimacy and Amazement. All these have nestled in my soul, and though I am fully aware that I have not done them complete justice in my work, they have never ceased to be my guiding lights." Barragán's ethos seems to speak to the spirit of Latin American architects today, who feel a close connection to their continent, favoring local traditions over foreign-born trends in architecture. Houses here often seem a natural extension of the land on which they stand. Space presents

less of an issue here than in, say, Japan, where residences are bound to the tiny sites allotted in their urban settings; there is a sense of generosity in the relation of Latin American houses to their surrounding space and views. There is simply more land, and more sites that offer the "amazement" that Barragán longs for. Though beset by difficult economic and political situations, Latin America is a vast land of possibilities, home of the "magical realism" of Gabriel García Márquez, Jorge Luis Borges and Isabel Allende. Contemporary Latin American architects may not consciously aim to evoke Barragán's Beauty, Inspiration, Enchantment, Serenity, Intimacy and Amazement in their work, but they often spring from the land where a terrace can be open to the infinite, and their architecture reflects this innate sense of freedom and possibility.

Most of the architects featured in this volume, though famous within Latin America, have not become well known outside the region. This may be due to the very vastness of the continent, and its often fiercely local culture, but perhaps also to a hesitance on the part of European and American critics and publishers toward these "far-away" lands. Colonialist or even imperialist attitudes may not lurk as far in the past as we might hope. But again, the emergence of the internet as a universal tool for students of architecture around the world has certainly begun to have an influence on the availability of information concerning contemporary Latin American architecture.

BREAKING THE SIEGE

Among the architects who have marked recent Latin American residential architecture, five might be singled out for their different approaches and the significance of their work: Solano Benítez, Tatiana Bilbao, Alejandro Aravena, the studio WMR Arquitectos and Isay Weinfeld. Solano Benítez was born in Asunción, Paraguay, one of Latin America's smaller countries, in 1963. Benítez represented his country at the 2016 Venice Architecture Biennale with the project "Breaking the Siege," an arch made of brick, concrete, and steel erected for a period of ten days in the Central Pavilion of the Giardini. For this work he was awarded the Golden Lion for Best Participant in the International Exhibition "Reporting From the Front," for "harnessing simple materials, structural ingenuity and unskilled labor to bring architecture to underserved communities." For Alejandro Aravena, curator of the Biennale, this pavilion is part of an effort "to reverse the idea that the Biennale only deals with issues that are of interest to other architects...by identifying problems that every citizen can not only understand but actually have a say in." Among his residential projects, the LA Farm House, in Santani, Paraguay, stands out—a large brick structure with an unexpected and relatively severe presence. The architect also designed his own offices in Paraguay with the kind of economic austerity that he has become known for. "Almost 20 years ago, with roughly $5,000, which we produced with much effort, we faced a difficult choice between two supposed necessities, to buy two good computers complete with the mirage produced by the desires of virtual existence, or with the same budget, to physically build our offices." The office was built with thin brick walls and low-density wooden boards in the place of a ceiling.

PART OF THE HILLSIDE

Tatiana Bilbao, born in Mexico City in 1972, has made her mark on the architectural scene in other ways. Before founding her own firm, Tatiana Bilbao S.C., in 2004, she was an Advisor for Urban Projects at the Urban Housing and Development Department of Mexico City, and was a Professor of Design at the Universidad Iberoamericana. Her office, which manages projects in China, Spain, France, and Mexico, was selected as one of the top ten emerging firms in the 2007 *Architectural Record* Design Vanguard. She curated the Ruta del Pelegrino (with Derek Dellekamp), a 117-km (73-mile) pilgrimage route through Mexico's Jalisco mountain range, from Ameca to Talpa de Allende, along which numerous architects created stopping points and small buildings. She often collaborates with other artists and studios, including Christ & Gantenbein and HHF Architects in Switzerland, Dellekamp Arquitectos in Mexico, ELEMENTAL in Chile, and Ai Weiwei's FAKE Design in China, inserting Mexico into the realm of cutting-edge international work. She is unafraid of experimenting with architectural tradition; while her Casa Ventura (p. 30) was made with concrete and geometric forms, it broke many Modernist rules. A Modernist approach might have sought to flatten this site and make it uniform. Instead, Tatiana Bilbao consciously sought to build a house that was part of

the hillside—in her own words, to "grow from it and become part of the composition of the natural environment." Even more contrary to the strictly geometric approach of Modernism, Bilbao also states that the design is inspired by fungi that grow on trees and "somehow become part of them."

HALF A HOUSE AND MORE

Before winning the prestigious award himself, Alejandro Aravena was a member of the Pritzker Prize jury between 2009 and 2015. He has been an International Fellow of the Royal Institute of British Architects since 2010. His projects include the Mathematics, Medical, and Architecture Schools at the Pontifical Catholic University of Chile, in Santiago, along with the campus's Siamese Towers and the Anacleto Angelini Innovation Center. Outside of Chile, he has built facilities at St. Edward's University in Austin, Texas, and a building for Novartis in Shanghai. In addition to this considerable body of work, Aravena has made significant contributions to architecture's impact on welfare issues, through social housing projects undertaken by his group ELEMENTAL. The Quinta Monroy, a complex developed to house a hundred families on land they had illegally occupied for decades in the heart of the city of Iquique, was Aravena's first experiment in what he calls "half houses." Because local government programs only offered enough funding to construct homes around the size of a studio apartment, ELEMENTAL provided residents with basic housing units: a two-story, two-bedroom home, with roof, kitchen, and bathroom—plus an equivalent empty space next to it. This gave residents decent living conditions, with the option to build on the second half of their property as and when they became financially able. The growing number of interesting projects such as this in Chile in recent years may in part be due to its economic situation: between 2003 and 2013, though real growth averaged almost 5% per year (despite a slight contraction in 2009 due to the global financial crisis), approximately 14% of the population was below the poverty line in 2013. Architects have stepped in to address the problem. It is estimated that, across the continent, one in five Latin Americans lives in a state of chronic poverty.

It may not be surprising that Alejandro Aravena chose Solano Benítez for the Venice Biennale, as they share a dedication not only to architectural innovation, but also to addressing the real problems of Latin American architecture and housing. The wealthy can of course afford spectacular beachside houses, giving architects opportunities to exercise creative freedom, but Aravena and Benítez, like just a few other major architects in the world, such as Shigeru Ban with his emergency relief work, are also putting their talent at the disposition of disfavored populations, really making a difference through their work.

CABINS ON A CLIFF, PALACE IN THE CITY

WMR Arquitectos, founded in 2005 by Felipe Wedeles Tondreau (1977–), Jorge Manieu Briceño (1976–), and Macarena Rabat Errazuriz (1982–), is a Chilean practice that creates spectacular private vacation homes from low budgets—these works are a study in contrasts. Their Cabanas Pura Vida (see pp. 206-13) inverts the stereotype of the cliff-top beach house by partially burying cabins and then cantilevering them over the steep slope, framing views of the ocean. With the architecture "discreetly incrusted in the landscape, hardly noticeable from above," WMR treats the relation of the house to the site with particular originality, defying the Modernist aversion to digging into the ground. The architects also make reference to traditional Chilean ideas of outdoor space, which given the climate often participates in residential spaces, while carefully protecting privacy and views of the site itself.

At the other end of the continent, in Brazil, Isay Weinfeld has designed a large number of expansive houses like the Casa Deck (pp. 170-77). Though the site area is restricted by its urban setting, through clever landscaping and multiple stories the architect develops an inner world where there is space for gardens that are contiguous with the house and extend its interior volumes. Born in 1952, Isay Weinfeld is at the height of his career and has worked on numerous other building projects than his houses—including the Hotel Fasano (São Paulo, 2001-3, with Marcio Kogan). Showing the international appeal of his work, Weinfeld was called on to design the new Four Seasons Restaurant in New York by Edgar Bronfman Jr. and his associates. Now located at 280 Park Avenue for its reopening in late 2017, the restaurant, a nearly mythical New York establishment, was long on the upper ground level of the Seagram Building, also on Park Avenue, designed by Ludwig Mies van der Rohe and Philip Johnson, completed in 1958.

A KIND OF MAGIC

These five architects offer a glimpse of the range and breadth of the creativity that flows through contemporary Latin American architecture as it is deployed in homes by the up-and-coming architects of the region. The houses in this volume are grouped according to the type of sites on which they are built: The mountains, cities, coastlines, and forests of this vast and varied continent. Latin American architects have approached the challenges presented by these environments, and embraced the advantages that they offer, in different ways. As is perhaps the case elsewhere in the world, there is no truly dominant style in contemporary Latin American architecture, and it may even be a perilous exercise to try to identify just what links Latin American architecture to the continent. It is true, however, that spaces that are both covered and open to the exterior are almost omnipresent here, as is a close link to the earth and to topography. These elements are inextricable from the nature of the continent—its lush scenery and particular climate. While the imported European Modernism has surely left its mark in Latin American architecture, Latin American architects have developed their own character, and have also influenced contemporary architecture throughout the rest of the world, to a greater extent than perhaps is acknowledged in the US or Europe. Concrete has been better mastered in Latin American than in many other developed parts of the world—Niemeyer proved this beyond a doubt. Though the vibrant colors of Barragán have largely been left in the past, a sense of his magic can still be felt in contemporary Latin American architecture—surely the magic of the earth itself.

[1] David de Ferranti, Anthony J. Ody, "Key Economic and Social Challenges for Latin America: Perspectives from Recent Studies," The Brookings Institution, August 1, 2006. The issues outlined in this paper remain current. https://www.brookings.edu/wp-content/uploads/2016/06/20060803.pdf, accessed on December 20, 2017.

ON HIGH GROUND

The 7,000-km (4,350-mile) long Andean mountain range is the second tallest in the world, dwarfed only by the mighty peaks of the Himalayas, and stretches across seven South American countries: Venezuela, Colombia, Ecuador, Peru, Bolivia, Argentina, and Chile. Mountains run throughout the continent from north to south, and the architects who work in these difficult regions seek to emphasize the precarious setting of their teetering mountaintop abodes while maximizing the magnificent views across the hills and down to the ocean beyond. A quick glance at the plans of this collection of houses confirms that rectilinear designs of varying complexity are the rule in this rugged terrain, with the curves of which Niemeyer was so fond all but absent. Elevations frequently show a direct relation to the topography of the particular sites on which houses sit; steep slopes are typically met either with a step-down logic or by cantilevering outward —in fact, understanding the design of these homes is often easier in elevation than in plan. At a time when nature seems to be retreating from our cities, many of those fortunate enough to have a house designed by a top architect choose to combine the comforts of modernity with the majesty of nature.

CASA RAUL

PAINE/CHILE/2007
Mathias Klotz

The relatively simple exterior style
of the Casa Raul is echoed inside,
though in a much lighter tone
of wood. The main open space
leads directly from the living area
to the bedroom.

The Casa Raul is a weekend residence located in the Andes mountains near the Aculeo Lagoon, 60 km (38 miles) from Santiago. The single-story house, built on the steep slope of the mountainside, was conceived as a continuous space in order to emphasize flexibility of living. The interior spaces, clad in pine panels, are essentially white, infusing the house with a sense of luminosity, contrasting with the house's dark exterior, designed to "merge into the landscape," according to the architect. The limited budget for this project demanded that the architect make effective use of basic materials and technology. The superstructure of the house, constructed of wood and steel, is supported by concrete pillars, cantilevered over the areas below, emphasizing its somewhat precarious setting and maximizing the distant views of the water. Drought and improper water management have unfortunately adversely affected the Aculeo Lagoon, but this house remains a striking outpost in the forested slopes above the water.

A simple railing with metal wires gives the impression that there is almost no barrier between the house and the view. The wooden picnic-style table accords well with the willfully unpretentious design.

Overleaf. The relatively narrow terrace seems to plunge residents directly into the natural setting, a feeling heightened by the cantilevered structure of the house, which hangs over a steep slope. The view of the forest in the foreground gives way to the lagoon beyond, and finally to the mountains.

CASA V

SOPÓ/COLOMBIA/2009
Giancarlo Mazzanti and Felipe Mesa (PLAN:B)

Casa V, which lies in the hills around Sopó, 39 km (24 miles) north of Bogotá in central Colombia, offers its residents continuous views of the surrounding mountains and the lake beyond through its innovative structure. Giancarlo Mazzanti, the architect, explains the organic inspiration behind the design: "Like the branches of a tree, the house falls over the site, and branches into two parts that separate the program into different heights: above, the social part, bridge, and terrace, and below, the part that contains private rooms and services. The main trunk is a library that starts the staggered journey from the house." The "branches" of the house are separated by an inner courtyard, and the differing heights on the sloped site allow the ground level of the upper section to be at the height of the roof of the other. This dynamic layout not only gives the entire house views of the surrounding mountains, but also allows for outdoor living on the roof areas. Approached from above, where there is space to park a car, the house initially appears as little more than a concrete-edged lawn, but steps leading down to the main open roof terrace with its wooden deck reveal the house below. The design of the house is deliberately simple and striking, with minimal embellishment; the roof terraces, for example, have only their low concrete edge, no railing.

Although the concrete and glass of the house would seem to separate it from the natural setting, the use of a partially green and accessible roof allows users to not only take in the broad view, but also to be in direct contact with the site.

The interior of the house, with
its stepped wooden platforms
and generous, angled windows,
gives a sense of architecture that
has accepted the slope of the
site as part of its condition and
raison d'être.

The rooftop terraces, in gravel and wood, have only a minimal ledge that separates residents from the broad view of the countryside. The upper terrace is planted very simply in grass, furthering the sense of unity with the natural setting.

"Like the branches of a tree, the house falls over the site, and branches into two parts that separate the program into different heights."

GIANCARLO MAZZANTI, ARCHITECT

CASA VENTURA

SAN PEDRO GARZA GARCÍA/MEXICO/2012
Tatiana Bilbao

This large family house is built on a sloped site in a suburb of Monterrey, in the town of San Pedro Garza García, and offers an impressive panoramic view of the city. The client wanted a single-story residence with a clear distinction between public and private spaces, as well as an orientation that would provide passive energy savings. The site reminded the architects of a photograph of Californian Modernist houses of the 1950s, taken by Julius Shulman, which formed the inspiration for their design. Each part of the design program is inscribed in a pentagon that is adapted or "deformed" according to the site and to the movement or uses of its residents. The resulting geometric plan nonetheless gives rise to forms that maintain a close relation to their natural setting. The flatter part of the site forms the base of the home's public spaces, while the private areas are perched atop the hilly topography. A spiral staircase connects the two zones. According to the architects, the design was also inspired by the fungi that grow on trees and "somehow become part of them." Exposed concrete "in its most apparent and natural form" was used to increase the sense of "belonging to the location." The house can be imagined as a kind of organic, albeit fundamentally geometric, excretion that emerges from the site, flowing over its contours while maintaining a sense of the presence of Modernist design and architecture.

The $2,000,000 development is formed from a series of interconnected blocks with a spiral stairway leading from the private areas to public ones. The house in a sense steps into and over the site, or rather emerges from it.

The entrance level of the house gives little hint of the dramatic rear side—rather here a calm horizontality is emphasized.

"We decided to use concrete in its most apparent and natural form, creating a sense of belonging to the location. The house builds up like another protruding cliff or like a fractal from the same slope."

TATIANA BILBAO, ARCHITECT

The skylit stairway combines feelings of enclosure and openness, a theme that is also clearly visible in the dining and living area. Full-height glazing contrasts with opaque concrete surfaces.

Overleaf. Hanging plants in the stairway soften the impression of hard surfaces, but tiled floors, wood cladding, and concrete walls and ceilings are the rule in this house.

HOUSE IN FUTRONO

LAKE RANCO/CHILE/2013
Izquierdo Lehmann Arquitectos

Skylights and angled white surfaces bring ample daylight into the house, while fully glazed walls permit continual views of the natural setting and the lake. The design is at once bold and rigorous in its attention to detail and the spatial experience it creates.

Located on the western shore of Lake Ranco, in the south of Chile, this vacation house has the capacity to host up to eighteen people. The major challenge of the project was to integrate the relatively independent parts of this compact villa. The main rooms are located on the upper floor, which has an "H"-shaped configuration within a nine-square grid, conceived to encourage a gradual movement from the outside to the center, and from there to each room. The architect states, "Each room is, to a certain extent, dependent on the overall system while simultaneously preserving its own independence—its own center. The structure...aims to balance the attributes of the building as a whole with the specific requirements of its parts." These parts are covered by a symmetrical four-pitched structure made of metal beams, directly supported on metal columns of different heights, according to the level of the sloped ground. The children's area, which is below grade (the natural level of the site), faces the lake, and throughout the house generous glazing allows residents to admire the panoramic view of the hillside setting while they live in comfort.

A sleek bathroom shares a continuous band of windows with the corner bedroom. The gamut of colors is limited to black frames, dark wood floors and doorways, and white ceilings and walls. Picture windows in the corner bedroom seen here give almost continuous visual access to the setting, a hill above Lake Ranco.

Overleaf. A covered wooden terrace has nearly uninterrupted views of the lake, with regularly placed steel columns giving an architectural rhythm to the space.

MOINHO VILLA

VALINHOS/BRAZIL/2014
WAY

The design contrasts a decidedly
rectilinear form with jagged rocks
from the site. To the right, the
house's sliding wooden shutters
can be seen in both the open and
closed positions.

Overleaf. The living and dining
area of the house opens entirely
onto both the central patio and
a rear garden. The exterior stone
walls are in the tones of the natural
rocks from the site.

The steep site of the Moinho Villa, studded with natural granite boulders, is surrounded by beautiful forest views, and WAY sought to seamlessly integrate the house into both its topography and naturally dramatic vista. Central to the design is a communal patio, conceived by the architects as the "house's heart," that links the main living spaces and cooking area together. Despite the uneven site, the house has a single story, achieved by suspending the main volume over the existing rocks; excavation of these boulders had to be carried out with explosives in order to create a garage level with the rest of the villa. The living room has large sliding glass panels on both sides, allowing the internal and external areas to merge, increasing the sense of the house's unity with its environment. Throughout the interiors,

cumaru timber floors, gray limestone, and ceramic tiles contrast with the natural stone walls constructed in the outside areas. The architects, concerned that the building be as sustainable as possible, installed a green roof along the whole span of the house in order to increase thermal insulation, as well as providing more green space for residents, and solar panels and gas provide energy. This was the first project built by WAY in Brazil, and the architects worked closely with the whole team on the site, overseeing the local labor force—which was not formally trained in modern construction methods—and collaborating with small family businesses that had little experience in developing non-traditional projects.

The smooth interior surfaces
contrast directly with the rough
stone walls outside. The wooden
underside of the house appears
to sit atop the existing rocks.

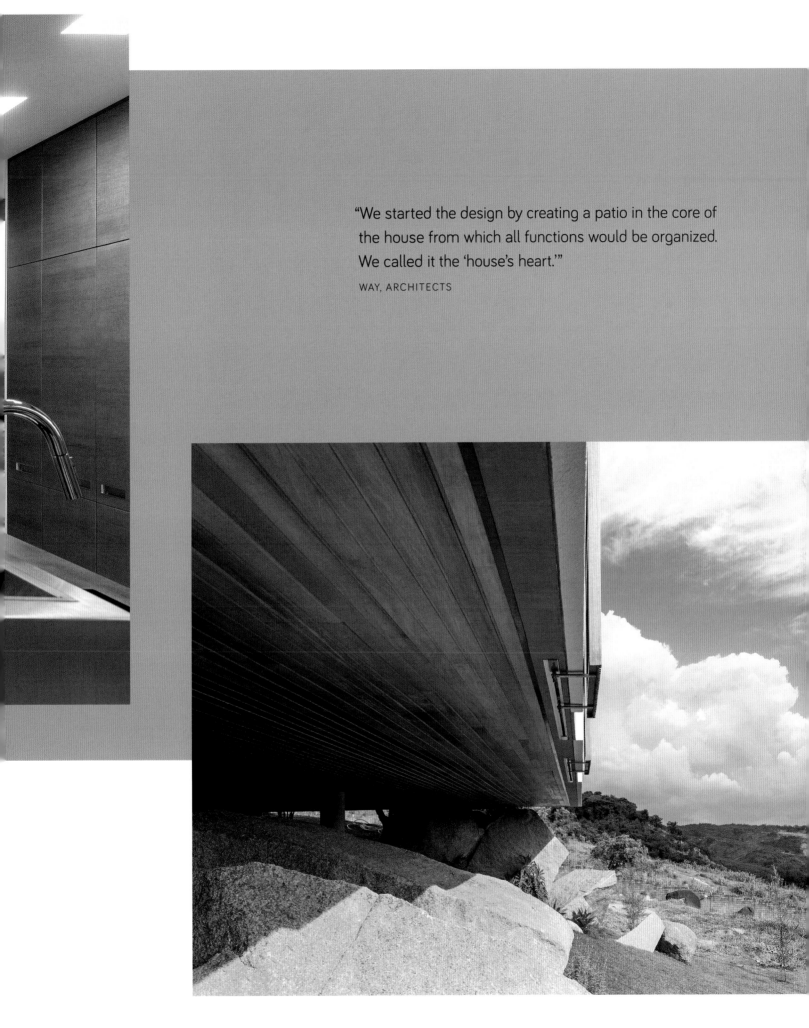

"We started the design by creating a patio in the core of the house from which all functions would be organized. We called it the 'house's heart.'"

WAY, ARCHITECTS

FINCA AGUY RETREAT

PUEBLO EDÉN/URUGUAY/2015
MAPA

The sheet metal exterior of the
house gives it an almost industrial
appearance, and indeed the
structure is prefabricated, but
the simplicity of the form adds a
sense of elegance and modernity
to the design.

The Retreat in Finca Aguy was assembled in a factory near Montevideo and then transported 200 km (125 miles) to Pueblo Edén, near Punta del Este, a popular resort city in the department of Maldonado. In order to facilitate the transportation of the prefabricated steel-frame structure to the site, the house essentially takes the form of a large rectangular box. It was installed near an olive grove as an "off-grid" meeting place for different members of a family during the holidays. This construction method was chosen for economic reasons, but also to reduce the impact of construction on the site and to minimize waste. The floor of the house is in garapa wood, while the walls are covered in Canadian pine. Sheet metal was used for the exterior of the house because of its low maintenance requirements. Glass doors offer a maximum capacity to open the house to the exterior in good weather. A longitudinal veranda made with lapacho wood (Brazilian walnut) panels can be adjusted for greater or lesser degrees of openness, as desired by the occupants. The house is designed to be entirely sustainable, equipped with its own waste treatment system, using water from the site, and using solar energy.

Canadian pine walls and garapa
wood floors give a natural warmth
to the interiors, while full-height
glazing puts residents in almost
direct contact with the rather wild
natural site.

CASA MA

TEPOZTLÁN/MEXICO/2016
Cadaval & Solà-Morales

Concrete ceilings, stone walls, and
high windows affirm the solidity
of the residence and echo nearby
cliffs, while also giving residents
broad views of the setting.

Overleaf. Full-height glazing
gives an impression of complete
openness to this living space.
A suspended concrete stairway
leads up to a low mezzanine level.

This residence is located on the outskirts of the same town as the Bungalow (see pp. 82–87), and is surrounded by mountains on either side, and neighbors in the opposite directions. The task of the architects, therefore, became to offer views of the mountains from the main spaces of the house while closing it in the direction of the neighbors, and define a protected perimeter in which the residents can fully appreciate the location. The house is conceived as three pavilions under a shared roof, with two covered patios. The design encourages the movement of residents along the perimeters of the house as opposed to concentrating it, in more typical fashion, through the interior courtyard. This is a willful variation on the theme of the "patio house." While they describe the outer perimeter of the house in terms of a certain "rigidity," the architects seek to overlay a

second sequence of "open and enclosed spaces; the exterior spaces (roofed patios) intersect the volume diagonally and break with the rigidity of the perimeter." The angled roof makes something of a bow to the dramatic natural setting, rising up at each end so that mountain views dominate the living space and bedroom; this effect is maximized by double-height glazing that makes the proximity of the mountains particularly evident from inside the house. Structural stonewalls, explicitly requested by the client, together with the dark metal frames of the windows, give a certain rough texture and hardness to the architecture that "reinforces the views and the power of nature." Here, as in the other work of the architects in Tepoztlán, the intimate relation of interior and exterior is paramount, with covered patios conceived to be usable even in rainy periods.

HOUSE AT LAKE RANCO

LAKE RANCO/CHILE/2014
Izquierdo Lehmann Arquitectos

This six-bedroom vacation house is located on a vast, sloped site above Lake Ranco in southern Chile. The house includes a main living and dining room, kitchen, playroom, garage, and a basement with a service apartment. The long, flat house is open to the north, offering views of the lake through a covered terrace. A glass corridor that runs parallel to the terrace on the south side of the house allows views of the garden and patio formed by the retaining wall of the site. The entrance is across a parking area on the west side of the house. The structure is formed by symmetrical lines of pillars that carry a series of parallel transverse beams, supporting the flat, gravel-covered roof. The wooden ceiling and roofing boards form a rigid diaphragm that binds the entire structure. All wooden wall and ceiling surfaces have a light stain that enhances the natural look of native redwood, while darkened laminated pine structural elements such as

The markedly planar design seems to fit perfectly into the hillside. The slope in front of the house is simply covered in grass that leads down to Lake Ranco.

the cladding provide an interesting contrast. The same redwood was used for flooring in the living area and bedrooms. The kitchen and the playroom have natural ceramic tiles on the floors. Retaining walls and the chimney are made of concrete with exposed gravel, as are the exterior pavements. At the lakeshore below, another similar but smaller pavilion with a covered terrace was built as a boat house and barbecue area. All the buildings are deliberately placed in order to take advantage of the natural landscape without disturbing it.

The living area is fully open on two sides, with a gray stone chimney on the inner façade. This gray stone contrasts with the wooden floors and ceilings.

ECOSCOPIC HOUSE

MONTERREY/MEXICO/2016
Manolo F. Ufer

The Ecoscopic House is located at the southern edge of Monterrey at the foot of the Sierra Madre Oriental mountain range. The architects took this location as their inspiration for the structure, which lies "between the natural and the artificial"—the city and the mountains. They imagine the house as "an assemblage of platforms of interexchange that capture the flux of crossing ecosystems." Such factors as exposure to sun and shadow, prevailing winds, surface water flow and storm runoff, as well as the patterns of movement of local wildlife, were analyzed as part of the design process. Interlaced slabs and beams made of reinforced concrete were used to create a structural enclosure with high thermal inertia, "capable of withstanding the drastic daily temperature fluctuations and seasonal thermal oscillations characteristic of the local climate." The walls are between 110 and 350 mm (4½ and 3¾ in.) thick, depending on their location. The house was "handcrafted" on site using steel, glass, and in-situ concrete. The architect acted here "as client, investor, structural engineer, contractor, site supervisor, and property developer." The majority of the open-plan ground floor serves as a living area, complemented by a covered porch that adds another public space, protected from the sun and rain, with panoramic views of the Huajuco Canyon. The private spaces of the house, including three en-suite bedrooms in addition to the master bedroom, occupy an upper level. From the master bedroom, residents can access a planted terrace with spectacular views of the mountains. The service area of the house includes the kitchen, with a pantry, and laundry room, and a two-vehicle roofed parking area—with additional open-air parking for another two vehicles—is nearby.

The Ecoscopic House is imagined as a kind of folding point of intersection between the nearby mountains and the city of Monterrey. Its angled presence seems to convey a sense of movement, despite the extensive use of concrete. The cantilevered, angled forms and the broadly glazed ground floor seem somewhat counter-intuitive, but the overall effect is fully mastered and coherent.

The interiors of the house confirm its exterior appearance, all of which can be related to the angled and overlaid forms celebrated in the 1988 exhibition "Deconstructivist Architecture" at the Museum of Modern Art, New York.

The roadside façade of the house announces its angled, glazed design, albeit in a slightly less exuberant way than the opposite side of the residence.

ALBINO ORTEGA HOUSE

TEPOZTLÁN/MEXICO/2017
Rozana Montiel

A weekend house, this structure was built entirely with local construction materials, beginning with a Texcal stone base. The architect wanted to introduce a sense of variety to the home, despite the constraints of the small site, varying effects between a closed façade and the open garden space. The central courtyard of the house has a square opening that is echoed in a square basin, the whole surrounded by rough stone walls, and punctuated by louvered wooden doors. Water is present both inside and outside the house, refreshing the spaces, filling them with humidity and sound. As is frequently the case in the region, the interior and exterior spaces interpenetrate freely, here modulated with large windows and wooden shutters. The main room of the house was conceptualized by the architect as a "floating" wooden structure on the second floor. A square pond marks the ground-floor hall space, "subtly appealing to the users' perception: the emphasis," says the architect, "is on the hues and textures."

An artful mixture of wood and stone gives an airy appearance to the house, whose ground floor is broadly opened to the exterior. Opposite, a pool reflects the structure, and below, the upper volume of the house seems to float above the lower level.

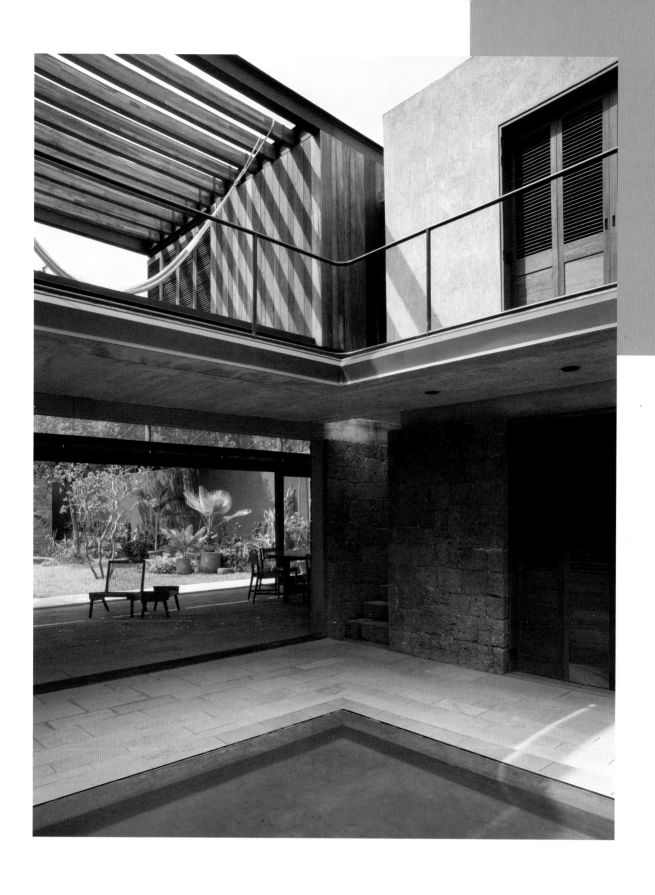

"The place can be experienced as a grand terrace with a luscious garden."

ROZANA MONTIEL, ARCHITECT

An upper-level wooden terrace is framed in steel, encapsulating the overall design theme: a contrast between closed and open surfaces. The architect also mixes references to indigenous architecture, such as the use of local stone and building methods, with modernity, expressed in steel and concrete.

THE URBAN CONTEXT

While vacation homes, or residences in scenic locations, tend to be broadly glazed so as to make the most of their surroundings, their urban counterparts are logically more closed, or open toward the interior rather than in the direction of views. This fundamentally changes the nature of the architecture. There is a certain complexity common to the projects presented here, but no singular style. Latin American architects do not have any fixed idea of what "modernity" looks like, though they surely have more freedom to make reference to their own traditions than the previous generation. Modernity was previously felt to be antithetical to tradition, in the spirit of the *tabula rasa*, but this is no longer the case, and architects in Latin America as well as elsewhere have sought to combine the past and the present. Indeed, site and the needs of specific clients would appear to be far more important factors in determining design than any consideration of an architect's origin. A sense of materiality, a willingness to boldly contrast materials—rough old stone against white steel, as in the case of the Casa Holmberg in Buenos Aires (pp. 100–5), or dark stone and steel juxtaposed with light-colored wood in the Casa Pareadas (pp. 118–25)—may identify these as Latin American homes, but it is clear that the architects would not be lost for ideas should they build in other parts of the world. Latin American architects have well and truly entered the international elite of their profession.

CASA TONALÁ

MEXICO CITY/MEXICO/2014
Jorge Gracia

The unusual façade of the house
combines an unsurprising ground
level with a large upper volume
that includes a vast stained-glass
window. The inner stair makes
use of a sculptural railing that
might bring to mind the world
of Antoni Gaudí.

The Casa Tonalá project involved the total remodeling of a
house in Mexico City's historic Colonia Roma. The exterior
and interior were entirely renovated, and new volumes
added to the existing structure. The architect deliberately
preserved the differences between the historic building and
the contemporary additions, most visible at roof level. The
design takes flat pilasters in the corner and center of each
façade as the guide for the spaces generated inside the
structure. A gray-painted base runs around the façades,
interrupted only by the main door and the garage entrance.
Windows and doors use a geometric trellis design with a
diagonal accent that echoes the interiors, where angular
walls "provoke feelings of openness" within the confines
of the small site. The architect placed an emphasis on the
continuity between the "original essence of the house" and
the finishes used in the new spaces. The reinforced concrete
slabs and annealed red clay walls of the original structure
are contrasted with a light system based on vertical steel
columns and galvanized steel walls for the new volumes.
This light system was devised to avoid having to reinforce
the older building and also to obviate the risk of any aggressive
competition between the old and the new. Despite its urban
setting, the house also makes considerable use of outdoor
terraces that, when open, broadly form the interior areas.

Stained glass is used throughout the house. The large window visible from the street is seen here inside the double-height living area, which in turn opens onto an enclosed patio. The main internal stairway, with its geometric balustrade, can be seen from the kitchen.

Opposite, the enclosed patio, and right, the upper part of the stairway with its light metal structure visible. Stone, wood, and plaster form the basic palette of materials, with black steel highlights.

Overleaf. The outdoor terraces of the house are made to feel an extension of the interior with full-height glazing.

CASA HOLMBERG

BUENOS AIRES/ARGENTINA/2016
Estudio Borrachia Arquitectos

Espacio
monitoreado
por cámaras
de seguridad.

A section of old brick wall together with a planar white metal door form the ground-floor façade. Above this, a vertical, metal cage rises, containing the main volume of the house. Inside, a stairway runs along the street-facing side of the upper metal-and-glass block. Wooden floors give a visual warmth that might otherwise be lacking in the white metal composition.

This three-bedroom, three-level house, named after Calle Holmberg, the neighborhood of northern Buenos Aires in which it is situated, was designed for a family of four—a young couple with two children. The interior floor plan is flexible, having no permanent divisions. The design includes three gardens, all overlooked by the rooms on the ground floor: One toward the street that provides access; one at the back with a private swimming pool; and another with a "wet patio" that is used to control the house's temperature. A water circulation system using tubes and perimeter pipes allows for the exchange of hot and cold water, depending on exterior temperatures, using two ponds—the cool "wet patio" in the shade at ground level and the other one on the roof, warmed by the sun. Solar panels can also be used to heat the water in winter, creating a "warm mattress" that obviates heat loss and reduces energy consumption. The external tube system is also used to support climbing plants, "transforming the façade into a kind of vertical garden," and the unique microclimate created by this system has encouraged a proliferation of local species.

An upper-level bedroom opens onto the stairway and white metal façade of the house, filtering out views of the street but allowing natural light to flood the space. The architect makes reference to an industrial vocabulary, but the refined details of the interior design take the realization elsewhere.

CASA DIAZ

VALLE DE BRAVO/MEXICO/2011
PRODUCTORA

"From the lake, the house is perceived as a composition of rectangular elements with large glass surfaces; a series of typical modernist volumes, stacked in a dynamic configuration."

PRODUCTORA, ARCHITECTS

A stairway next to the house, and indeed the architecture itself, steps down to the water. Though it is surrounded on three sides by other residences, the house succeeds in creating a kind of privacy.

Valle de Bravo is located on the shore of Lake Avándaro, 156 km (110 miles) south-west of Mexico City. The Casa Diaz is composed of three elongated rectangular volumes, with one side of each open toward the lake. These volumes, stacked in a zigzag pattern atop the sloped site, create a series of open terraces and irregular, sheltered patios. This configuration, together with the main garden and the fully glazed façades of the volumes, makes a direct connection between the house and the waterfront. A tiled roof, wood, natural stone and a façade finished in plaster were used to confer a "regional character" to the dwelling, in line with local building regulations.

Overleaf. The interior of the house gives little hint that neighbors are not far away. Covered outdoor spaces and full-height sliding glass doors make the connection between interior and exterior almost continuous.

CASA EUCALIPTOS

TLAJOMULCO DE ZÚÑIGA/MEXICO/2014
MO+G

The Casa Eucaliptos, located to the south of the city of Guadalajara, was built in two phases, and the design was largely guided by administrative restrictions and solar orientation. The walls of the house were rotated to protect it from the sun, while the front façade is essentially blank, hiding the main entrance. This entrance is placed at the juncture of the day and service areas near the point of vertical circulation. The design finishes are a reflection of the structural system of the house, with the architects placing an emphasis on the simplicity of the materials, "that produces warmth and a sense of traditional construction." Leaving the rough, white-painted brick visible not only reduces costs, but also bears witness to the quality of local workmanship. The architects further explain that "the roughness and heterogeneity of the walls will be strengthened with the patina of time from rain, dust, and vegetation," so that the relationship between the house and its setting will only deepen over time.

The entrance of the house is effectively hidden by the "blind" façade, while the main living space is opened to the exterior with generous glazing.

Material contrasts enliven interior spaces: An arched brick ceiling (left) and a ribbed wooden one (opposite) draw the eyes of visitors upward. Stone and wood seem to come together in a natural way.

CASA PAREADAS

SANTIAGO/CHILE/2014
Smiljan Radic

This pair of "semi-detached" houses was built for two friends, one of whom is a painter, and the other a sculptor. They bought the site together and imagined building two separate and different houses, but architect Smiljan Radic proposed instead to pair the houses and to develop overlapping volumes, each surrounding a central garden. Radic took the typical configuration of houses built in the 1960s in his native Chile as his source of inspiration, and here shows a great capacity for architectural innovation within constraints that are quite specific. The reinforced, rectilinear concrete houses, of roughly equivalent size, are placed together in a way that makes the distinction between the houses less readily evident, but nonetheless preserves the privacy of each owner. A large, blank volume of concrete marks the street side of the structure, giving it a sense of separation from its neighbors, as well as presenting an interesting visual contrast to the series of small isolated volumes that otherwise cram the neighborhood. The interiors are simple in design and seek to profit from sunny conditions around the patios. The interiors are clad essentially in poplar, contrasting with the relatively rough black concrete surfaces of the exterior. There is a sophistication in the glazing and gardens, which creates an intimate atmosphere despite the houses' urban setting. Here, clearly, the architect has redefined the meaning of the "semi-detached" house, so familiar in England and elsewhere, but not in this form.

Radic makes a willful play on the black concrete façades of the house and its green enclosed garden, or with the much lighter wooden floors and ceiling of the continuous living/dining/kitchen spaces.

Overleaf. Dark metal and light wood are directly related to each other in the interiors, with views of the garden never far away. Despite the simplicity of the interior designs, a sense of luxury permeates the two houses.

TROPICAL GREENERY

Perhaps more than any other continent, Latin America has broad areas that are tropical and thus covered in luxuriant vegetation. This is of course true in Brazil, where Isay Weinfeld's Casa Yucatan (pp. 128–35) is located, and where Jacobsen Arquitetura built the SM House (pp. 144–51). Building in a tropical climate has direct implications for the architect, who is particularly free to blur or even remove the distinction between interior and exterior. Imagine luxurious living space that is open to the evening air of the tropics, or thoroughly modern forms enveloped in the vegetation of the jungle. The symbiotic relationship of the site and the architecture—the natural and material—redefines residential architecture. This kind of relationship can be seen in the Casa Terra, designed by Bernardes Arquitetura (pp. 160–69); whether seen from ground level or in aerial images, this house seems fully integrated into its remarkable natural setting in Brazil. Of course, architects may also willfully play on the contrast between the built and the natural; though Oscar Niemeyer saw the curves of his native Brazil as a source of inspiration, today's talented residential architects appear to feel that rectilinear designs are more in the spirit of the moment, the curves and meanders of nature acting as accompaniment, rather than mirror, to their work.

CASA YUCATAN

SÃO PAULO/BRAZIL/2009
Isay Weinfeld

Located in the Jardim America area of São Paulo, the Casa Yucatan was designed for a young couple of art collectors and their three children. The architect chose to deploy seven box-like volumes of different sizes, and with different finishes—fair-faced concrete, precast concrete plaques, whitewashed bricks, and rough stucco—asymmetrically at the front of the site, leaving space in the rear for a garden. Progressing from the entrance, a long wall covered in black aluminum plates—the garage block—leads to the kitchen and then to the dining-room blocks. Four further blocks contain the daughter's and guest bedrooms, the sons' bedrooms, the master bedroom, a TV room and a gym. Isay Weinfeld explains, "The 'scattered' layout leaves generous spaces between the volumes that, topped by a wood-covered ceiling slab, not only serve as circulation, but also shelter the main living room, the family room and the works of art." A pool extends from the dining area toward the back of the site. Generous covered terrace areas allow for the kind of indoor-outdoor living that is possible in the climate of São Paulo, with average temperatures in the range of 19° to 25°C.

The box form of the dining room sits above the water, seeming to float there. The frameless glass walls heighten the effect.

Wood floors and ceilings provide a sense of continuity throughout the interior spaces, while minimalist furnishing contributes to the sensation of large, open volumes that give way to the exterior setting.

Overleaf. The house blocks contrast full-height glazing with the large, closed cubic volume on the right. The pool on the left, aligned with the dining space, almost seems to enter the house itself.

ILHABELA HOUSE

ILHABELA/BRAZIL/2010
Marcio Kogan

The simple furnishing of the house
is in harmony with the architecture;
the dining table and benches seem
to reproduce forms of the house
itself at a smaller scale. In the
broadly opened public space, in
which a rough stone wall contrasts
with the otherwise smooth surfaces
of the interior, the dining and living
areas are separated by a long, low
piece of furniture.

The more private areas of the house form a kind of bridge over the generous, open public areas, where interior and exterior no longer seem to have any distinction between them.

The Ilhabela House sits on Feiticeira Beach and carries the name of its location, an archipelago just off the shore of the state of São Paulo. The architects sought to integrate elements of Asian architecture that would be familiar to the clients, who follow Hinduism and Buddhism; a large statue of Buddha overlooks the garden, sitting in a specially designed niche. The open-plan ground floor unites the living, dining, and kitchen areas. The private spaces of the house on the upper level incorporate bamboo louvers that allow air to circulate while keeping temperatures down, a vital concern in this hot, humid region.

A "floating" stairway climbs the stone wall near the lower-level living space. The large external bamboo shutters of the house protect the private areas in the open position.

Overleaf. When the bamboo shutters are closed, the house offers a rather enigmatic wooden façade, delineated by sharply defined bands of concrete. They generously overhang the patio area, enabling exterior living in variant weather.

SM HOUSE

GUARUJÁ/BRAZIL/2014
Jacobsen Arquitetura

Generous wooden overhangs
shelter the terrace from both sun
and rain. The rich tones of the wood
contrast with the gray stone base
of the house and blend with the
natural setting.

The long terrace and wooden wall and ceiling that greet the garden bring to mind the kind of precision and juxtaposition of materials seen in Japanese temples.

The broad wooden staircase contrasts with the natural stone wall and leads to very large wooden doors giving access to the outdoor terrace. The interior living space can be opened entirely when the weather permits, and centers around a spacious seating arrangement surrounding a low wooden table.

The architects used rare Freijó wood, rough stone, granite, and glass to construct this beach house on the north-eastern shore of the state of São Paulo, at the edge of the Atlantic Forest. Indoor and outdoor spaces flow freely into each other, taking advantage of the tropical climate, while eaves that have a 4-m (13-ft) overhang above the indoor-outdoor living area shelter residents from the rain and fierce sun. The plan of the house is rectangular and the roof is flat, with glulam beams—a natural alternative to steel or concrete. Access to the house is at the lower level that forms a stone-walled base for the house. Two suites and a home theater are also located at this level.

The vertical bands of the wooden
wall cladding meet the lines of the
wood ceiling, creating a luxurious
enclosure from which the natural
setting can be seen through
floor-to-ceiling glazing.

"The concept desired for this project was to create
an elementary architectural composition combined
with advanced techniques in wood construction."

JACOBSEN ARQUITETURA, ARCHITECTS

CASA CUBO

SÃO PAULO/BRAZIL/2012
Marcio Kogan

As its name implies, this house assumes the form of a cube, which contains all functions of the residence. Large, perforated metal panels form a "skin" around the house that can be opened at ground level, revealing the living room to the patio and pool; the architects envision the common area as "a rip in a concrete box, totally integrated with the garden." Operable windows in the bedrooms, television room, and office on the upper floors provide natural ventilation, while retaining the metal paneling system that filters light. Sliding glass panels further open or close these spaces. The system of metal and glass panels is embedded in the walls, giving the homeowners full control of lighting and ventilation. The top floor houses part of the home's infrastructure, and also a small outdoor living area and a garden terrace, with a spectacular view over the surrounding area. Echoing the simple geometric form of the house itself, a limited palette of materials is employed: The façades are made of rough concrete—shaped using handcrafted wooden forms—and metallic panels, whose color is reminiscent of the concrete itself. Specially designed ceramic tile floors form a continuous decorative feature in the public spaces. At night, because of the perforated metal paneling, the house glows from within.

The apparently heavy volume of
the house sits on just two corner
columns, freeing the living space,
which is seen here entirely open to
the exterior. The metal panels on
the ground floor can be adjusted
to form openings of various
sizes, or entirely closed when
the homeowner desires privacy
or shade. The lower part of the
house in particular glows in the
dark, as does the pool.

CASA TERRA

ITAIPAVA/BRAZIL/2015
Bernardes Arquitetura

The Casa Terra located in Itaipava, about 230 km (140 miles) north-east of the city of Rio de Janeiro. The essential structural character of the Casa Terra is determined by parallel walls made of pigmented concrete that run perpendicular to the house's central circulation axis. The house is further formed by its flat roof, and the high, thin columns that support it, creating a transparent central pavilion space. Large glass windows and openings along the circulation path further allow for frequent contact between the interior and exterior of the house, and so the greenery of the setting is visible from one end of the residence to the other. The interiors are marked by the extensive use of wood and generous natural light, brought in partially along the edges of the high floating ceiling of the main living space. The landscaping, by Daniela Infante, brings to mind Oscar Niemeyer's House at Canoas (1951), designed as his family home, in the city of Rio—but in this instance, the sensuous curves of Niemeyer have been replaced by a rectilinear vocabulary where transparency is of the utmost importance.

The stone walls of the house and its surrounding landscaped greenery set it apart from its beautiful natural setting, but also integrate it, making its presence in the environment seem quite natural.

The house alternates glazed and
opaque, pigmented concrete walls.
This generates a relatively simple
shed-like configuration that offers
both broad views of the mountains
and a certain enclosure for privacy.

An aerial view reveals the composition made up of strict rectangles in the green setting. A long swimming pool stands in front of the house.

"The closure between the vertical (walls) and horizontal (slabs and floor) planes is made with large glass panels that dilute the visual boundaries between the house and the landscape."

BERNARDES ARQUITETURA, ARCHITECTS

In the main living area, metal columns lift the roof above the alignment of the pigmented concrete walls, allowing light in not only from the sides but also from above.

The living and dining spaces form continuous volumes, extended by the outdoor terrace when the sliding glass walls are opened.

CASA DECK

SÃO PAULO/BRAZIL/2010
Isay Weinfeld

The uppermost level of this three-story house, which sits on a steeply sloped hillside, acts as the main entrance and contains the residence's public and service areas. Outside, a dense garden leads to a swimming pool, then an open lawn and, finally, a large veranda with hammocks hanging from the stilts supporting a roof slab, whose top serves as a solarium overlooking the city. Beyond the veranda and along its whole length, an ample living space is divided into two lounge areas and a dining room by wooden partitions. The bedrooms, set on the intermediate level, feature sliding doors opening onto a wooden deck that extends toward another lawn that continues to the outer wall. At the lowest section of the land, the eastern façade opens into the garage and service entrance to the lower street.

Wooden ceilings and walls give warmth to the interior. In the distance, the lights of the city are visible.

The glazed walls of the living area slide fully open, allowing residents to be indoors and out at the same time. Stone floors contrast with the wooden ceilings.

The architect orchestrates different materials and colors to enliven and enrich the spaces of the house. Here, interior and exterior come into almost direct contact.

Overleaf. Columns create a generous covered outdoor space.

MARIA & JOSÉ HOUSE

ITU/BRAZIL/2016
Sérgio Sampaio

The dark coloring of the house
and its crisp delineation stand in
stark contrast to the natural site.
The apparent weight of the upper
volume is made to hover above the
open parking area on thin pilotis.

Built between 2014 and 2016, this large house is located on a steeply sloped site, with an 8-m (26-ft) difference in height from one end of the plot to the other. Despite the steep curvature of the land, the clients wanted a single-story structure with full accessibility for older people. The main functions of the house—social, leisure, and private—are located in a single prismatic volume that stands above the natural ground level on metal pillars. The service areas and garage are located below this main volume, taking advantage of the natural slope. The façades of the house are relatively closed, but a large internal patio admits ample natural light. A reinforced concrete pool extends from the garden into the main volume of the house "as a strategy to integrate leisure activities into the social life of the house." The house was built with cross-laminated timber panels over a metal structure, and with sustainability in mind—rainwater is collected for the irrigation of the gardens, solar panels on the roof are used to heat water, and special laminated glass reduces heat gain. Cross ventilation is employed and sliding panels, partitions, and roof areas increase the potential for open contact with the exterior.

From the parking port,
a simple ramp runs directly
up into the house.

Wood, concrete, and glass combine
to create a rather hard-edged
ambience that is accentuated
by the sharply defined shadows
cast by the vertical panels.

Within the house, minimal furnishing complements the strong lines of the architecture. In the dining space, sliding glass walls offer full contact with the exterior.

Overleaf. At nightfall, the house displays one glazed corner that stands out against the otherwise opaque façade. Low steps lead to the entrance area, where spotlights highlight the dark surfaces.

COASTAL RETREATS

Few residential environments offer the kind of encounter with limitless space the way a coastal site can. A number of countries in Latin America boast spectacular seaside settings that talented architects have tamed for their private clients. Along the Chilean coast, Mathias Klotz's Casa Bitran (pp. 190–97), Cristián Undurraga's Casas del Horizonte (pp. 198–205), and, in a slightly less grandiose fashion, the WMR's Cabanas Pura Vida (pp. 206–13) all benefit from, and are shaped by, their stunning surroundings. Here, the architecture is turned toward the ocean, facing the immense horizon. The waterside Vallarta House, by Ezequiel Farca and Cristina Grappin (pp. 214–21) in Mexico, has a more urban feeling, while in Costa Rica the Casa Cinco, by Robert McCarthy (pp. 222–27), contrasts stone walls and sloping roofs with an apparently unspoiled shoreline. These houses generally share substantial glazing and openings that allow residents to see, and very possibly to feel, the majesty of the sea, escaping the urban world in order to regain contact with the climate, the wind, and the smell of the water.

CASA BITRAN

BERANDA/CHILE/2009
Mathias Klotz

Set on a 30° slope by the beach of Cachagua, the
Casa Bitran seems to hang above the beach, offering
spectacular views from every point including the roof.
Anchored at the rear, the residence sits amid the site, as
if reclining to survey the seascape beyond. The house has
two levels, with the public space forming a kind of indoor-
outdoor terrace on the upper floor. This blurring of the
distinction between indoor and outdoor space is rendered
possible by the climate and is achieved with a number of
sliding elements, including large windows and a wall that
separates the kitchen and dining-room space. The private
areas are thus on the lower floor, with more than 50% of the
space set below grade. A series of skylights provide natural
light for these areas. The overall plan is a composition of
rectilinear forms that tends toward a square shape. Although
concrete, glass, and steel are used extensively for the main
structure, the interior spaces employ wood and stone that
gives a warmer feeling.

The volume of the house wraps around the rear to leave the front, facing the ocean, entirely open. An upper terrace, which can be closed to the elements, is complemented by a lower one. A swimming pool lies further down the slope.

Suspended concrete stairs lead down to the private living space. This cosy area seems to sit just above the waves, with broad glazed openings that allow the wind and sun into the house.

Overleaf. This lower-level bedroom has its own terrace, as well as sliding glass walls that remove any barrier between residents and the presence of nature in all its splendor.

CASAS DEL HORIZONTE

ZAPALLAR/CHILE/2009
Cristián Undurraga

These two residences in Zapallar, a fashionable seaside resort on the central coast of Chile, are set on a steep slope 25 m (82 ft) above the Pacific Ocean that offers views of the sea and, on a clear day, of the port of Valparaíso, 60 km (37 miles) to the south. Referring to the dramatic natural setting, the architect states, "The formidable sum of stimuli offered by the site demanded a radical architectural decision, setting a new order in the landscape without introducing any characteristic in contradiction with the forces expressed by nature." The architect therefore made a conscious effort not to impose these houses, which are of similar size, on the already spectacular landscape. Rather, he chose to focus on what he calls the "length" and "magnitude" of the buildings. The houses were constructed by excavating two large cavities, their stone walls echoing the rocks that naturally unfold onto the lush oceanfront.

The powerful rectangular forms of the architecture provide for ample glazing and thus for unimpeded views of the ocean. A stairway leads down to the garden, and beyond to the water.

"Length and magnitude were the main themes to start the project.
Used as a strategy to integrate the building to the sensitivity of the place,
length to cover the site, and magnitude to contain the landscape."

CRISTIÁN UNDURRAGA, ARCHITECT

The strong presence of the house is marked on the upper side by a long pool that separates the slope from the flat patio areas. The concrete walls have openings that give views through the house and toward the ocean.

The houses sits above the main
living areas very much like a
powerful bridge, linking two sides
of the slope, leaving space for the
residents to fit into this exposed
landscape at the ocean's edge.

The houses perch on these walls by means of a bridge, creating intimate and protected spaces below. By using the natural features of the site in this way, the architect blurs the boundaries between architecture and landscape; the excavated courtyards are imagined as a kind of primitive, natural world, upon which the overlying bridges impose a rational order. The structural aspect of the project is based on 44- and 48-m (144- and 158-ft) long post-tensioned reinforced concrete beams that are supported by three pillars. Floor slabs are hung from these elements with steel posts. The main materials employed in these low, rectangular houses are reinforced concrete, glass, stone, and steel. The enclosed ground floor includes the living, dining, and kitchen spaces, as well as a patio with a reflecting pond, landscaped with local ornamental plants. The bedrooms and bathrooms are upstairs. Large windows not only allow spectacular views, but also, through a system of mobile lattices, help to cross-ventilate the structure, taking advantage of the constant sea breezes to cool the houses.

CABANAS PURA VIDA

TUMÁN/CHILE/2013
WMR

WMR have had considerable success building relatively low-cost and yet spectacular residences on the coasts of Chile. Here a blackened wood frame provides both shelter and an unexpected degree of architectural inventiveness, given the budgetary constraints imposed on the project.

WMR designed this group of cabins for a couple who love music and surfing. The complex is made up of the couple's main residence and three cabañas that are available for rent; maintaining a degree of privacy, while taking advantage of a steep site's ocean view, was therefore of paramount importance. The architects decided to sink the cabin structures into the earth, so that the natural ground level is similar to that of the roofs, with excavated entrances that lead to the living spaces. The identical orientation of the sunken volumes means that despite their close proximity, each one has a good deal of privacy. As the semi-buried structures are placed at the top of the slope, their terraces introduce more than a mild sense of vertigo—in fact two of the cabins are suspended over the cliff. The wooden structures are based on an orthogonal 2-m (6½-ft) module, made primarily from glass and local pine. A *quincho*—a typical Chilean outdoor space consisting of a traditional barbecue, a hot tub, and a swimming pool—overlooks the garden and the buried volumes. The first section of these cabins is lit only by skylights, until visitors reach the main bay window and terrace overlooking the mountains and the sea, facing the setting sun. The overhead sun is blocked by a lattice of narrow wooden slats set in a regular orthogonal pattern. The main house is divided into two primary parts—night and day zones—separated by a middle axis that successively offers interior and exterior spaces.

Wood, both artificially blackened
for the exterior frame and naturally
tinted for the interiors, defines
the space. The simplicity of the
architecture is evident, as is the
furnishing of the light-filled rooms
and terraces that it defines.

"The three similarly elegant volumes, discreetly incrusted in the
landscape, are hardly noticeable from above except for the light
that comes out through the circular skylights when night falls."

WMR, ARCHITECTS

Overleaf. A large circular skylight
complements the large windows
and sliding doors, while the
orthogonal black wooden frame
partially shields a broad terrace,
fitted out, as seems appropriate,
with a suspended hammock.

VALLARTA HOUSE

PUERTO VALLARTA/MEXICO/2013
Ezequiel Farca + Cristina Grappin

The waterside site of the house
is clearly privileged. The angled
composition is complemented by
a curving pool to the rear. A green
roof completes the design.

The Vallarta House is located in the Pacific Ocean resort of
Puerto Vallarta. The furniture and decorative elements of
the house were chosen and designed to integrate seamlessly
with the architecture, which the architect compares to 1950s
Modernism. The use of natural stone and concrete passively
cools the house in summer, because of their thermal mass.
The home's walls and rooftops thus insulate it from heat,
reducing the need for artificial ventilation, and also serve
to integrate the house with the landscape. The two-story
structure has the public areas on the lower level and
the private spaces above, and includes a fitness center,
home theater, two hot tubs, a fire pit, eight bedrooms,
and numerous multi-functional gathering spaces both
indoors and out. Each room has floor-to-ceiling windows
that open onto private terraces, offering spectacular views
of the ocean.

Interior spaces are bright and airy, and glazed walls provide stunning views of the water. The lower-level living area extends seamlessly from interior to exterior, giving residents a sense of unity with the ocean and mountains in the distance.

Overleaf. The upper terrace hangs far out above the lower living space, allowing the broad expanse of the view to penetrate deep into the inside of the house.

CASA CINCO (C5)

GUANACASTE/COSTA RICA/2015
Robert McCarthy

Casa Cinco (C5), on the Pacific coast of Costa Rica, was designed as a second residence for the architect Robert McCarthy and his family of four. McCarthy applied local building principles to his own structure, taking inspiration from the domestic forms—and what he refers to as "volumetric primitivism"—of nearby coastal homes. The exterior of the house, with its stone walls and broad pitched roof, therefore has something of a traditional aspect, although the high narrow windows introduce a touch of modernity. The main entrance is via a stone courtyard, with obscure gates; the house seems totally engulfed by its wild surroundings, overlooking a rough beach from its dense jungle—it is constantly under assault by the encroaching forest and the harsh, salty wind from the coast. Regional stone and wood, as well as custom-cast bronze, were the main materials, and extensive work was done to create custom detailing and furnishings for the house. The house plan is simply organized in the form of four stone cubes with two large wooden roofs, and the design relies on deep shade to encourage natural ventilation.

The rather formal lines of the walls and roofs of the house, inserted into its luxuriant forest setting just above the sea, contrast with the curving unspoiled beach in the distance.

"The result was intended to be timeless and durable and not fashionably light in structure."

ROBERT MCCARTHY, ARCHITECT

The house's interiors, with high ceilings and full openings, seem to be more obviously in harmony with its location that the exterior implies. Ceiling fans are used to give some movement to the warm, humid air.

CASA GHAT

ZAPALLAR/CHILE/2015
Max Núñez

The modern, concrete volumes of
the house face out to the ocean.

The interiors of the house make
surprising, sculptural use of concrete,
with a staircase seeming to hang
unsupported over the lower floor.

Built on a 25° slope facing the Pacific, the design and internal layout of the Casa Ghat was essentially determined by the client's desire to create a continuous volume on the uneven site, leading down to the ocean. A reinforced concrete slab roof, supported by fifteen concrete columns of different sizes and shapes, adapts the inclination of the slope. Both structural needs and spatial aspects determined the irregular geometry of the supporting columns. Each column thus becomes a singular element, defining a particular point in space and framing the landscape in different ways. The architect points out that the sloping design thus avoids any monotony despite the free plan space. Four lighter volumes cladded in Lenga wood mark the surface of the roof and the space below it, while seven internal concrete stairs connect the living space with a terrace. Three of these volumes contain private rooms; the fourth, and smallest, allows direct access to the terrace from the interior. These volumes are situated under, beside, and above the roof, creating ambiguous relations between private and public areas of the house.

CASA L4

COSTA ESMERALDA/ARGENTINA/2015
Luciano Kruk

The architect built this house for himself on Costa Esmeralda, 13 km (8 miles) north of Pinamar and four hours from Buenos Aires. A screen of maritime pines lies between the neighborhood where this house was built and the seacoast, respecting the 200-m (650-ft) setback required by provincial regulations. The site slopes gently in the direction of the ocean. Exposed concrete was chosen for the house because of its resistance to local weather conditions and easy maintenance, and also because its color and texture harmonize with the natural surroundings, a key concern for the architect. A dark, semi-covered space leads visitors to the bright open area of the main living zone, located at the center of the design, with the four bedrooms at the exterior corners. Another seating area on the roof allows residents to admire the natural setting. At the lowest point of the terrain, the house hangs 2 m (6½ ft) above the ground. The side walls have essentially opaque surfaces with horizontal "cracks," while the front and the

The uninterrupted upper concrete volume of the house is suspended over a glass-walled ground level. The rough casting of the concrete seems to make it fit better into its wooded setting.

rear are entirely transparent. The concrete stairs were conceived as an autonomous sculptural element, and the walls that separate the bedrooms from the central area are treated "with the same expressive plasticity, thus generating niches and protruding volumes that function as fixed furniture," according to the architect.

"We built a box amid a slice of nature and, by letting the exterior flow in and out through it, we made it a constituent part of its environment. Thus, the box and its surroundings merge and vibrate in consonant harmony."

LUCIANO KRUK, ARCHITECT

The concrete shell of the house wraps around the glazed volume. A concrete staircase cuts through the main living space, separating the kitchen and dining areas.

Overleaf. Skylights above the showers and central staircase introduce natural light to the otherwise quite enclosed volume.

FOREST HIDEAWAYS

Far from the expansive vistas that surround mountain and seaside houses, the woods impart to the residences nestled within them a wholly different, more intimate mood. Indeed, the close proximity of dense vegetation provides a sense of security and a connection to nature that is undeniable. Cazú Zegers' Casa Granero in Chile (pp. 244–49) captures this connection by making full use of wood for both the exteriors and interiors. Fernanda Canales and Claudia Rodriguez's Bruma House in Mexico (pp. 250–57), on the contrary, employs black concrete to great effect; the stone-like walls of the house do not seem out of place in a forest environment, but evoke an almost natural, though unexplained, presence. Mixing the two approaches, the Casa Cher by BAK Arquitectos in Argentina (pp. 258–65) wraps a concrete shell around a glass, wood, and metal interior, with wooden decks pierced to allow existing trees to remain integral to the site. In this case, as in others, nature appears to enter these houses, to become one with residences that nonetheless remain modern and comfortable.

CASA GRANERO

KAWELLUCÓ/CHILE/2004
Cazú Zegers

Continuity between the interior
and the exterior of the house is
achieved by the uniform presence
and coloring of wood. There is an
obvious warmth in the design,
and thus a heightened sense of
being in a "forest hideaway."

The Casa Granero seeks to create a close relation between its wooden forms and the surrounding landscape, taking its inspiration from the traditional forms of local barns specific to southern Chile. The architect has designed a number of houses that have as their theme the agricultural shed, but creates contemporary representations of these agricultural buildings. Set slightly off the ground on a low concrete base, the house has horizontal wooden slats that cover its external surfaces, aside from areas where generous glazing is present. The use of wooden planking on the walls and roof generates a continuous envelope that has space for very tall interiors, with attics and balconies facing into the forest. The interior and furnishings, made on site, are also entirely in native coigüe wood, with a stairway and mezzanine partially occupying the double-height space.

Interior spaces make use of double height, with both an enclosed mezzanine space and open volumes. Furnishings are in rough wood, with a wood-burning stove in the center of the residence.

"This Barn House is a contemporary reinterpretation
of the traditional shed from the south of Chile."

CAZÚ ZEGERS, ARCHITECT

BRUMA HOUSE

VALLE DE BRAVO/MEXICO/2017
Fernanda Canales

Links between the blocks are
glazed, but the blocks themselves
are mainly opaque.

The nine blackened volumes of the Bruma House sit
around an irregularly paved stone courtyard. Their
placement takes into account every tree that existed
on the site, as well as the views, orientations of the sun,
and existing vegetation offered by the site. The volumes
comprising the kitchen, dining room, living room, master
bedroom, and children's bedroom are connected with
covered, but glazed, walkways. Two separate volumes,
including two guest bedrooms, service areas, and
the garage, form the opposite side of the central patio.
Each space is linked to the central patio and opens at
the opposite end, meaning their interior spaces are
completely open to the landscape while maintaining a
sense of privacy within the complex. The living room and
one guest bedroom also have roof terraces. Each volume
has a different height that corresponds to its topographic
situation and to an identified spatial hierarchy. The master
bedroom is located on the upper floor, above the children's
bedroom and above a studio that opens up to a private
terrace. A larger studio, with direct access to the roof terrace
above the living room, is located above the dining area.
An exterior staircase running alongside the main patio
leads to the other roof terrace, which faces a mountain
to the east. The architect explains, "The project highlights
each volume's independence, but also the interaction and
sequence that exists between them." Black concrete, wood,
stone, metal, and glass form the entire palette of materials
used. The design and its use of black concrete tend to make
the house almost disappear against the heavily wooded
backdrop of the site.

Inside the house, concrete gives way to warmer wooden walls, ceilings and a stairway.

Wood alternates with black concrete and gray surfaces in the interior spaces. Large windows allow residents to look out into the surrounding forest.

Overleaf. Seen from a distance, the house is almost entirely subsumed by the surrounding vegetation, its black concrete blending into the forest beyond.

CASA CHER

MAR AZUL/ARGENTINA/2010
BAK Arquitectos

This small summer residence at the edge of Mar Azul forest, on the eastern extremity of Argentina, was designed for a couple with two teenage children, who wanted to take advantage of views of the pine and acacia woods. These views are assured by generous glazing and wooden terraces that extend from the house toward the forest. Half-levels were used as a response to the topography of the site, as the structure is partially buried in a dune, typical of the area. This enabled the creation of a semi-sunken courtyard and a double-height space. The concrete and glass shell that comprises the main volume of the house highlights these different levels. Although modern materials are used, the simplicity of the design is such that residents are placed in almost direct contact with the natural environment. This is due to the full-height windows, but also to the way that the house sits on the land, with its protruding wooden deck pierced to allow existing trees to remain.

The concrete shell of the house and its wooden terrace are lifted off the sloping site, with trees allowed to continue to grow through the decking. The main living space opens on both sides, giving residents the impression that they are sitting in a protected environment in the midst of the forest.

Wood-formed concrete and a subtle
juxtaposition of colors and surfaces
give the house a warmth in keeping
with the surrounding woods.

Wooden terraces extend from the
house and quite literally begin to
take in the forest. The incorporation
of existing trees into the very
fabric of the house affirms the
link between the architecture
and nature, otherwise achieved
by the full-height glazing.

CASA EN EL COPE

EL COPÉ/PANAMA/2012
Patrick Dillon

The east wing of the house seen
here includes minimal furnishings
and the living and dining space,
as well as open-air decks that look
out over the forest.

This house near the Omar Torrijos National Park is built
on a mountainside, with a single topographic elevation
and all rooms oriented to mountain views. The informal
tent- or shed-like S-shaped structure was built on concrete
foundations, with polished concrete floor slabs. A steel
superstructure has a roof that slopes toward the entrance
courtyard, which contains a reflecting pool. The west wing
of the house contains four bedrooms and bathrooms, while
the opposite wing contains the kitchen, dining room, living
room, and three open-air decks projecting from the house
and suspended above the valley. The north, south, and
east façades have large glass or screen walls with doors and
windows that open in the direction of the mountain views,
while the western façade consists mainly of fixed wooden
louvers. "It's about the sensorial experience," says the architect,
"where you let yourself go and get into that natural rhythm
as the light changes and the breezes come in—it makes
you aware of being alive. That is the test of good design—
you forget about the architecture and enjoy the moment."
All decks, façades, doors, and window frames were made
with recycled wood retrieved from demolished structures
at the former US Air Force base at Fort Howard, at the
southern entrance to the Panama Canal.

The reflecting pool seen above is located near the entrance to the house. The external wooden decks are as informal as the house itself, allowing residents to live at their own rhythm in harmony with the natural setting.

"I've always looked at blurring the distinction between inside and out—here, with the climate, we can make do with just a roof, as long as we can deal with mosquitos."

PATRICK DILLON, ARCHITECT

CASA GUNA

LLACOLEN/CHILE/2014
Pezo von Ellrichshausen

Concrete stairs lead up from the ground-level terraces to the residence floor. This almost ceremonial entrance gives the house an unexpected solemnity.

The Casa Guna occupies a narrow site, set between a hillside and an area of eucalyptus trees facing a lagoon, in Llacolen, not far from Concepción, Chile. The architects chose forms and materials intended to articulate these contradictions in the topography. The main part of the house—a large concrete upper level resting on a smaller base—is set well above the ground. This concrete form has regularly spaced rectangular openings. The upper floor, arranged around a central patio, has four separate modules on each of its four sides. Overhead apertures at the center of each enclosed space and at the ends of the circulation paths emphasize the vertical aspect of the layout. The ground floor houses the day-to-day functions. Its square plan, divided into four equal quadrants, is cut out at the north corner where a stairway rises, creating "a visual and functional shortcut between the upper patio and the edge of the lagoon." The four walls of the patio act as Vierendeel girders resting on the podium. The concrete surfaces have a coarse texture from the formwork boards and a diluted black patina. Though the house appears massive and imposing because of its concrete volumes, and stands out as being apart from the natural setting, it seems ready to be covered with vegetation and offers light-filled, almost serenely floating views of the wooded landscape and water.

The upper-level living spaces have wide openings that allow views of the water and the natural setting. The quadrilateral form encloses the central upper courtyard.

SUSTAINABLE HOUSE

QUITO/ECUADOR/2014

Luis Velasco Roldan + Ángel Hevia Antuña

This simple wooden house is set slightly off the ground in a wooded setting among mature trees. The design of the Sustainable House was provoked by a concern that the abandonment of traditional building techniques has led to the creation of architecture that ignores local climate, economics, and social conditions. The architects therefore focused on utilizing innovative construction techniques and integrating the latest technologies, incorporating natural thermal insulation, solar capture systems through greenhouse effect, ventilated façades, and vegetable roofs in their design. A rock and concrete foundation with a steel pillar design is topped by a eucalyptus structure, and the walls and slabs of the essentially prefabricated house were filled with pumice stone after the installation of pipes. The ventilated exterior wall is built of Ecuadorian laurel boards, and the green roof covering comprises a layer of insulating and draining pumice stone between two layers of geotextile on double asphalt waterproofing. A layer of black soil and humus covers the roofing materials. The architects state that their "research is centered on the use of natural thermal insulation, solar capture systems through greenhouse effect, ventilated façades and vegetable roofs."

The grassed roof of the house is pierced to allow an existing tree to become part of the design. The kitchen and dining area is simple and has a large sliding glass door that allows it to open entirely.

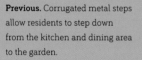 **Previous.** Corrugated metal steps
allow residents to step down
from the kitchen and dining area
to the garden.

The interior finishes and furnishings
are simple and bright, and arranged
around the existing tree that grows
right through the house.

CASA NIDA

NAVIDAD/CHILE/2016
Pezo von Ellrichshausen

With its upper, glazed level lifted
high off the ground, the house
seems an echo of the surrounding
pine trees.

Built in Navidad, a town on the central coast of Chile, this unusual design, which gets broader as it rises, is described as "concentric and non-directional" by the architects. It has eight continuous columns and eight other columns that step up in a regular way. This darkened reinforced concrete grid is complemented by native wood for the platforms, furniture, and window frames. The monolithic design encloses a dense framework of different levels connected by a spiral staircase. Despite the house's relatively high structural density, transparency is imposed through the use of floor-to-ceiling glazing, creating the sense that the surrounding forest is very near. A flat wooden roof even allows residents to emerge above the trees, and to see the Pacific Ocean in the distance. Explaining the design, the architects state, "From the top, the visual relationship with the inferior floor is imperceptible, to the point of canceling any contact with the natural ground. This veiled logic of an inverted gravitational adjustment (a classical 'entasis') timidly emerges on top of the surroundings foliage."

CASA PÁJARO DE PLATA

PLAYA NEGRA/COSTA RICA/2016
John Osborne

Located on a mountaintop in the remote beach town of Playa Negra, this vacation home for a New York couple was inspired by local vernacular construction that, in the architect's opinion, inserts itself into what Gilles Clément calls "the third landscape"—going with, rather than against, natural conditions. The project seeks to encompass the entire site and thus, according to the architect, has an "exploded," or perhaps more clearly a fragmented, floor plan, set up on a stone platform in a clearing that offers views of the surrounding countryside. The fragments of the plan are connected by terraces that recall a Mesoamerican past. Outdoor decks and a pool are arranged around a covered seating area, and its roofs stretch between the structures to the limits of the materials employed.

The unusual design combines its fairly solid base with lightweight roofs and elements such as the rectangular pavilion. The house is divided into a "sleeping unit" and a "social unit."

"The absence of glass, filtering of natural light, and play with the wind, do not allow for separation between house and its landscape."

JOHN OSBORNE, ARCHITECT

In the social area, the kitchen is marked off by a wooden floor and wall. The louvered windows provide aeration and ample light.

Overleaf. The kitchen and dining space, separated from the private volume, opens entirely to the elevated swimming pool and nearby barbecue area. The private area is to the rear in this image.

CASA RECREO

VALLE DE BRAVO/MEXICO/2017
Fernanda Canales

Inside, full-height windows, wooden ceilings, and stone floors are handled in a manner that is related to tradition but remains modern. A large fireplace dominates the living space.

The Casa Recreo is designed as a series of interconnected pavilions with asymmetric but repetitive roof designs, which vary in height, echoing the nearby Valle de Bravo mountains. A central patio links the main access, public spaces, bedrooms, and service areas. Another patio, facing the forest, connects the bedrooms to a set of studios. A large terrace allows the public spaces to open up to the landscape, where the living and dining areas have views to both the open surroundings and the central patio. Bedrooms and the breakfast patio, which are located to the east and south, receive morning sun, while the living and dining space inside the house, as well as the kitchen and outdoor dining area on the south and west sides of the house, get afternoon sun. The living space and kitchen open onto a terrace where there is a swimming pool. Although this is a single-story house, the height of interior spaces varies according to their function because of the inclined roof. Local materials, including gray stone, roof tiles, and wood, were used throughout, with an emphasis on craftsmanship in particular for the walls, floors, and roof.

Wooden ceilings and floors accentuate the surrounding views of the forest, a harmony maintained by the rough stone of the patios.

Interior space becomes fully
exterior with the opened folding
windows. Stone and wood are
orchestrated in a fairly rustic
and solid form.

HOUSE PLANS

CASA RAUL
pp. 14–21
180 m² (1,940 ft²)

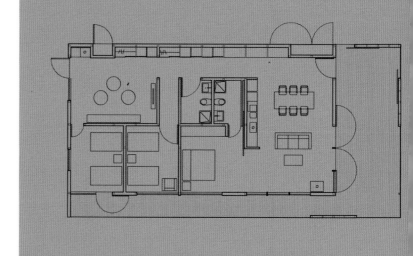

CASA V
pp. 22–29
220 m² (2,370 ft²)

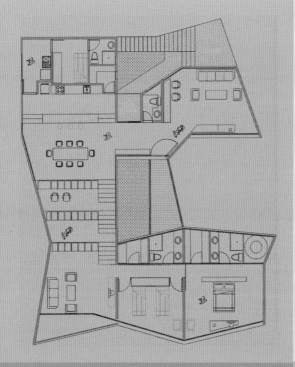

CASA VENTURA
pp. 30–39
854 m² (9,190 ft²)

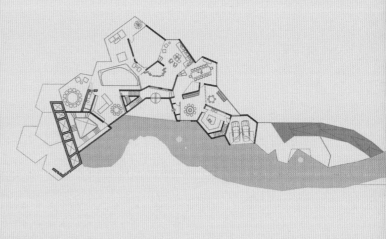

HOUSE IN FUTRONO
pp. 40–47
464 m² (5,000 ft²)

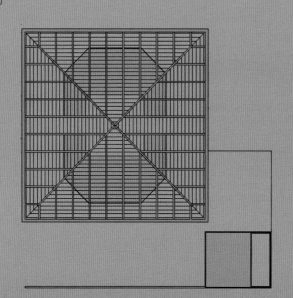

MOINHO VILLA
pp. 48–55
420 m² (4,520 ft²)

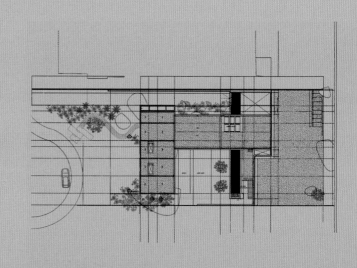

FINCA AGUY RETREAT
pp. 56–61
115 m² (1,240 ft²)

CASA MA
pp. 62–67
300 m² (3,230 ft²)

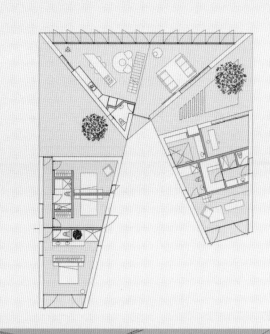

HOUSE AT LAKE RANCO
pp. 68–73
floor: 594 m² (6,400 ft²)

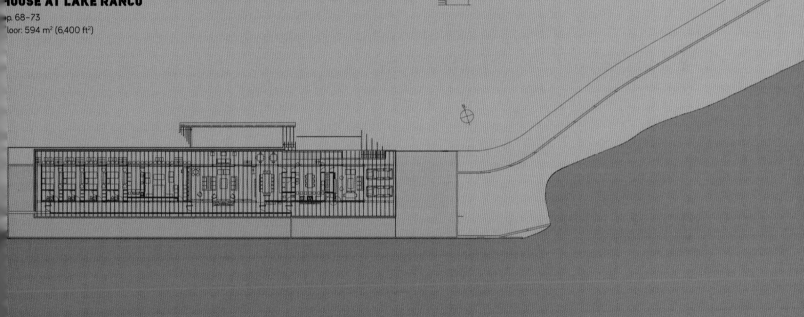

ECOSCOPIC HOUSE
pp. 74–81
650 m² (7,000 ft²)

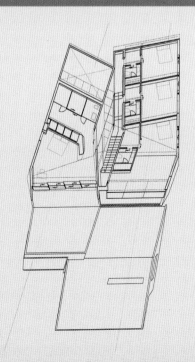

ALBINO ORTEGA HOUSE
pp. 82–87
405 m² (4,400 ft²)

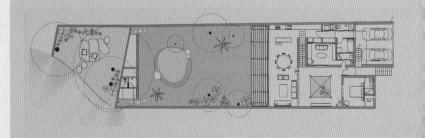

CASA TONALÁ
pp. 90–99
550 m² (5,920 ft²)

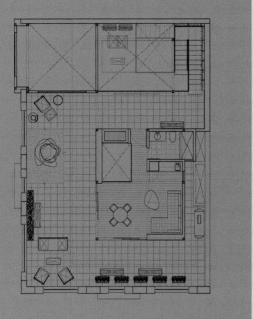

CASA HOLMBERG
pp. 100–5
170 m² (1,830 ft²)

CASA DIAZ
pp. 106–11
450 m² (4,850 ft²)

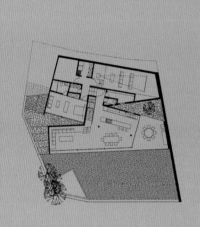 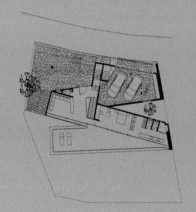 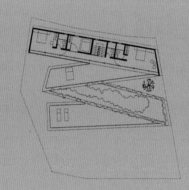 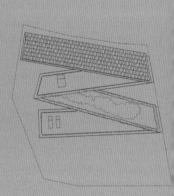

CASA EUCALIPTOS
pp. 112–17
220 m² (2,370 ft²)

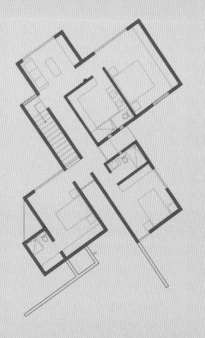

CASA PAREADAS
pp. 118–25
245 m² (2,640 ft²) and 240 m² (2,585 ft²)

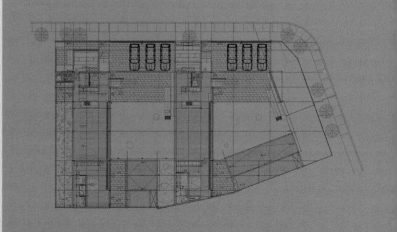

CASA YUCATAN
pp. 128–35
915 m² (9,850 ft²)

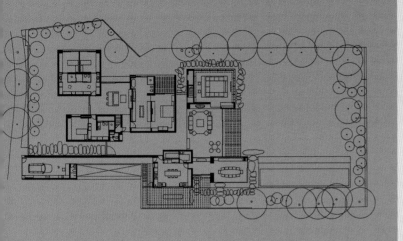

ILHABELA HOUSE
pp. 136–43
430 m² (4,630 ft²)

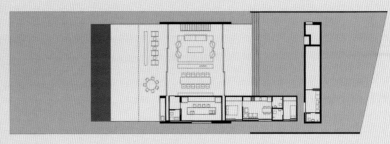

SM HOUSE
pp. 144–51
453 m² (4,875 ft²)

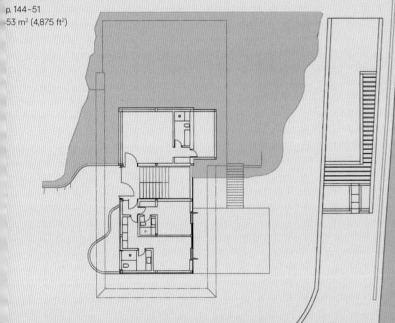

CASA CUBO
pp. 152–59
540m (5,800 ft²)

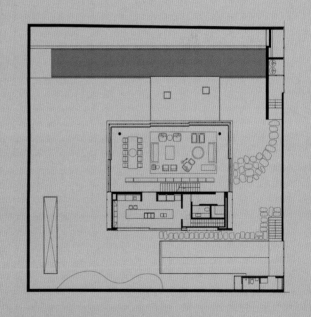

CASA TERRA
pp. 160–69
1,000 m² (10,760 ft²)

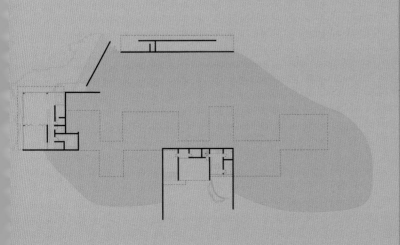

CASA DECK
pp. 170–77
1,249 m² (13,500 ft²)

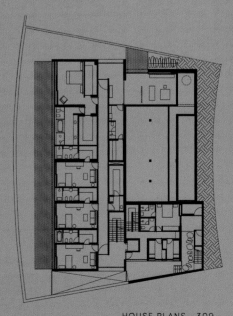

MARIA & JOSÉ HOUSE

pp. 178–87
1,350 m² (14,530 ft²)

CASA BITRAN

pp. 190–97
340 m² (3,660 ft²)

CASAS DEL HORIZONTE

pp. 198–205
433 m² (4,660 ft²) and 491 m² (5,285 ft²)

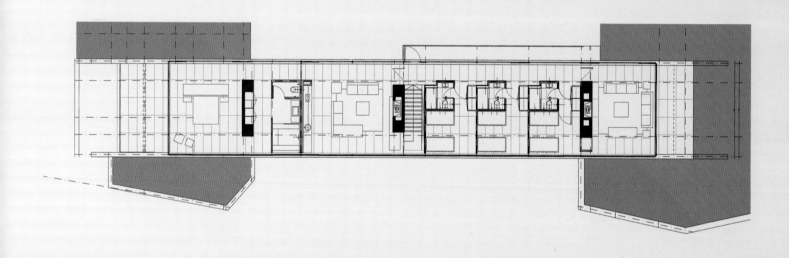

CABANAS PURA VIDA

pp. 206–13
180 m² (1,940 ft²)

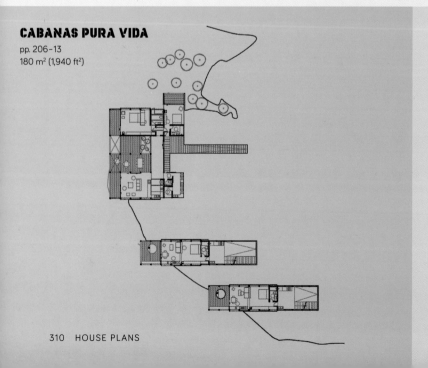

VALLARTA HOUSE

pp. 214–21
3,000 m² (32,290 ft²)

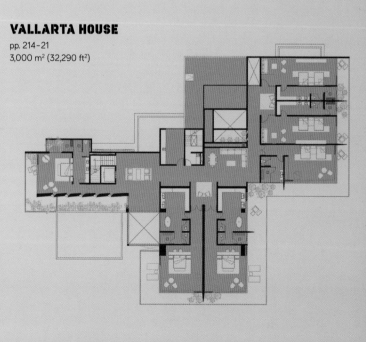

CASA CINCO (C5)
pp. 222–27
346 m² (3,725 ft²)

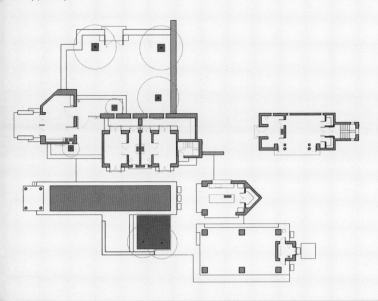

CASA GHAT
pp. 228–33
390 m² (4,200 ft²)

CASA L4
pp. 234–41
183 m² (1,970 ft²)

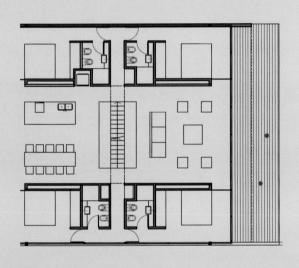

CASA GRANERO
pp. 244–49
116 m² (1,250 ft²)

BRUMA HOUSE
pp. 250–57
600 m² (6,450 ft²)

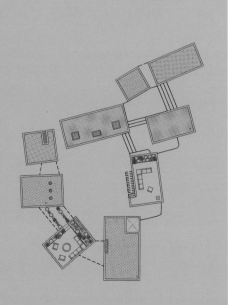

CASA CHER
pp. 258–65
105 m² (1,130 ft²)

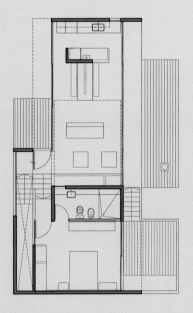

CASA EN EL COPE

pp. 266–71
520 m² (5,600 ft²)

CASA GUNA

pp. 272–77
410 m² (4,410 ft²)

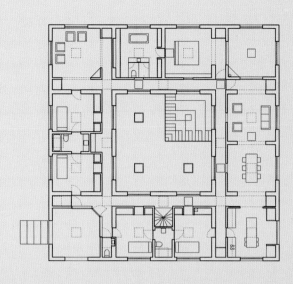

SUSTAINABLE HOUSE

pp. 278–85
49 m² (530 ft²)

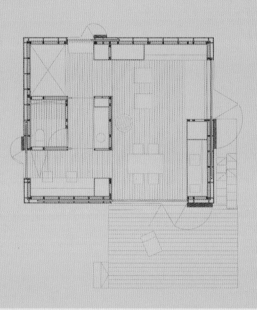

CASA NIDA

pp. 286–89
232 m² (2,500 ft²)

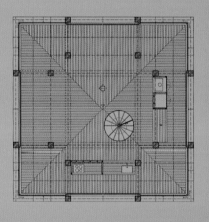

CASA PÁJARO DE PLATA

pp. 290–97
428 m² (4,600 ft²)

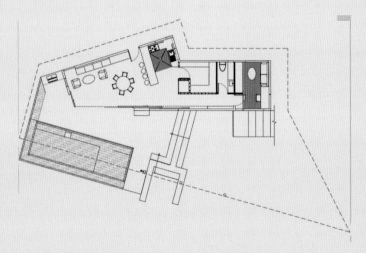

CASA RECREO

pp. 298–305
900 m² (9,700 ft²)

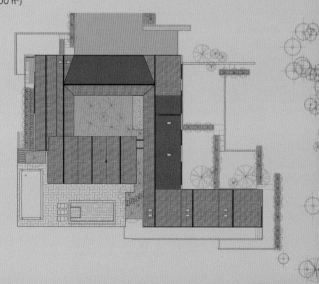

ARCHITECT BIOGRAPHIES

BAK Arquitectos
CASA CHER

BAK (Besonias Almeida Kruk) Arquitectos was established by María Victoria Besonías, born in Madrid in 1947, Guillermo de Almeida, born in 1945 in Buenos Aires, and Luciano Kruk, born in 1974, also in Buenos Aires, in 2000. Besonias was invited to speak at the 14th International Congress of Architecture in Monterrey in 2009 and the 2006 Biennial of Brasília and 2012. In 2012, the office split into two firms, Besonias Almeida and Luciano Kruk Arquitectos.

Thiago Bernardes
CASA TERRA

Born in Rio de Janeiro in 1974, Bernardes entered Santa Ursula College in Rio, but decided instead to engage in a self-taught career. In 1994, he opened his first office with Miguel Pinto Guimarães, and developed more than thirty residential projects between 1996 and 2001. After the sudden death of his father, Claudio Bernardes, in 2001, Thiago Bernardes stepped in as head of his firm, Bernardes + Jacobsen. In 2011, Thiago Bernardes created a new firm, Bernardes Arquitetura, along with Camila Tariki, Marcia Santoro, Dante Furlan, and Nuno Costa Nunes. They currently have offices in Rio de Janeiro, São Paulo and Lisbon.

Tatiana Bilbao
CASA VENTURA

Born in Mexico City, Mexico, in 1972, Bilbao graduated in Architecture and Urbanism from the Ibero-American University in 1996. In 2004 she founded her own firm, Tatiana Bilbao S.C., and in 2005 she co-founded the urban research center MXDF with Derek Dellekamp, Arturo Ortiz, and Michel Rojkind, and became a Professor of Design at the Ibero-American University. Her office was selected as one of the top ten emerging firms in the 2007 *Architectural Record* Design Vanguard.

Estudio Borrachia Arquitectos
CASA HOLMBERG

Founded in 2000 by Oscar and Alejandro Borrachia, this firm concentrates on academic work through the University of Buenos Aires, and IGEO, a design and research entity of the Faculty of Architecture of the University of Morón, Buenos Aires, as well as the planning and realization of buildings for UM and private work on houses such as the Casa Holmberg.

Cadaval & Solà-Morales
CASA MA

The studio Cadaval & Solà-Morales was created in New York City in 2003, and opened offices in Barcelona and Mexico City in 2005. Its founder, Eduardo Cadaval, was born in Mexico City in 1975, and gained his B.A. from the National University of Mexico in 2000, and a Master of Architecture in Urban Design from Harvard in 2003. He had previously worked with Abalos & Herreros in Madrid, and for Field Operations in New York. Clara Solà-Morales was born in Barcelona in 1975. She obtained her architecture degree from the School of Architecture of Barcelona in 2000, and a Master of Architecture from Harvard in 2003. Their work includes the Tepoztlán Lounge (Mexico, 2012), the Cordoba Housing Building (Mexico City, 2013), and the San Sebastian House (Buenos Aires, 2014). Both Cadaval and Solà-Morales are Associate Professors at Barcelona's School of Architecture, and have been visiting professors at the University of Pennsylvania and at the Massachusetts Institute of Technology (MIT) respectively.

Fernanda Canales
BRUMA HOUSE

Born in Mexico City in 1974, Canales received a Bachelors degree from the Ibero-American University in 1997, a Master in the History and Theory of Architecture from the School of Architecture of Barcelona in 2001, and her PhD in Architecture from the Superior Technical School of Architecture of Madrid in 2013. She is a respected curator and critic of architecture and design, and has published numerous books on Mexican architecture.

Patrick Dillon
CASA EN EL COPE

Born in the former Canal Zone in the Republic of Panama in 1952, Dillon obtained his Bachelor of Architecture from Arizona State University in Phoenix in 1976 and his Master of Architecture from Rice University in Houston in 1978. After studying, living, and working abroad for nearly twenty-five years, he returned to Panama to work in civil construction before creating his own architectural practice, ENSITU. He is also Director of Junglewood Design, and co-founder of Estudio Remoto, which focuses on tropical architecture for remote communities.

Ezequiel Farca + Cristina Grappin
VALLARTA HOUSE

Born in Mexico City in 1967, Farca is the creative director and CEO of the studio Ezequiel Farca + Cristina Grappin, having founded the firm in 1995. He studied at the Ibero-American University, completing a degree in Industrial Design in 1991. He also has a Masters degree in Large Scale Architecture and Other Environments from the Polytechnic University of Catalonia, Barcelona, and in 2012 he completed an MBA at the University of California, Los Angeles. Cristina Grappin joined the firm in 2016 as a business partner to coordinate the firm's Mexico City office. In 2017, the firm's restaurant project "Lucca" was awarded Best Gastronomic Design by *Architectural Digest México* as part of the annual Design Icons Awards, and in 2015 the studio received *OBRAS Magazine*'s Visionarios Award.

Jorge Gracia
CASA TONALÁ

Born in 1973 in Tijuana, Mexico, Gracia graduated from the Ibero-American University of Noroeste, Tijuana, in 1997. He briefly worked in the Sebastian Mariscal Studio in Massachusetts, USA (2003–4), before creating his own firm, Gracia Studio, in Tijuana in 2004. The studio's work focuses on providing architectural solutions that are highly efficient while retaining aesthetic appeal, incorporating and experimenting with a wide variety of materials and structural systems.

Paulo Jacobsen
SM HOUSE

Born in 1954 in Rio de Janeiro, Jacobsen studied photography in London before graduating from the Bennett Methodist Institute, São Paulo, in 1979. After partnerships with three generations of the Bernardes family in Bernardes + Jacobsen (see Thiago Bernardes), he founded Jacobsen Arquitetura in 2012 with his son, Bernardo Jacobsen, who had worked with Christian de Portzamparc and Shigeru Ban before joining his father's firm. The office currently has sixty projects in development, fifteen outside Brazil, and include residential projects alongside public works, such as the Rio Art Museum, completed in 2013.

Mathias Klotz
CASA RAUL, CASA BITRAN

Born in 1965 in Viña del Mar, Chile, Klotz received his architecture degree from the Pontifical Catholic University of Chile (Santiago) in 1991, and created his own office in Santiago the same year. His Central Library for Diego Portales University won both the Green Good Design Award in 2010 and a Holcim Award in 2011, and in 2015 he won an Award for Institutional Contribution to Architecture given by the Association of Architecture Offices of Chile.

Marcio Kogan
ILHABELA HOUSE, CASA CUBO

Born in São Paulo in 1952, Kogan graduated from the School of Architecture and Urbanism at the Mackenzie Presbyterian University, São Paulo, in 1976. He founded his own office, which renamed itself Studio MK27 in 2001, in the late 1970s. Kogan collaborated with Diana Radomysler on the award-winning Ilhabela House. In 2011, Kogan was selected to be an Honorary Member of the American Institute of Architecture, and in 2012 Studio MK27 represented Brazil in the Venice Biennale of Architecture.

Luciano Kruk
CASA L4

Born in 1974 in Buenos Aires, Kruk received his degree in Architecture from the University of Buenos Aires, 2000, where he subsequently taught until 2009. Between 2000 and 2012, he was a partner at BAK Arquitectos, receiving numerous awards during his time there, including the First Prize for an Individual Housing Project at the 2007 and 2009 CAPBA Biennials. In 2012, he founded his own firm, Luciano Kruk Arquitectos, and in 2015 he was chosen as a representative for Argentina in the 9th International Festival of Architecture and Urbanism, "Architecture Week Prague 2015."

Izquierdo Lehmann Arquitectos
HOUSE IN FUTRONO, HOUSE AT LAKE RANCO

Izquierdo Lehmann Arquitectos was established in Santiago in 1984 by Chilean architects Luis Izquierdo Wachholtz, born in 1954, and Antonia Lehmann Scassi-Buffa, born in 1955. They graduated from the Pontifical Catholic University of Chile in 1980 and 1981 respectively. Cristián Izquierdo, son of Luis Izquierdo, became a partner in Izquierdo Lehmann in 2012. He was born in Santiago in 1982 and studied architecture at the Pontifical Catholic University of Chile (graduating in 2008), going on to receive an MSc in Advanced Architectural Design from Columbia University, New York, in 2014.

MAPA
FINCA AGUY RETREAT

MAPA is a bi-national collective established in 2013 that works in Brazil and Uruguay. Its founding partners, Luciano Andrades, Matías Carballal, Rochelle Castro, Andrés Gobba, Mauricio López, and Silvio Machado were born and educated in either Brazil or Uruguay.

Giancarlo Mazzanti
CASA V, with Felipe Mesa

Born in 1963 in Barranquilla, Colombia, Mazzanti received his Diploma in Architecture from the Javeriana University (Bogotá) in 1987 and completed his postgraduate studies in the history and theory of architecture at the University of Florence (Italy, 1991). His built work includes the International Convention Center (Medellín, 2002); the Santo Domingo Library Park (Medellín, 2006–7); El Porvenir Social Kindergarten (Bogotá, 2008–9); the Four Sports Arenas for the South American Games (Medellín, 2009–10); and the Chairama Spa (Bogotá, 2009–10). His work in Medellín in particular has shown that contemporary Colombian architecture is indeed alive and able to improve living conditions for people who are not well off.

Robert McCarthy
CASA CINCO

Born in 1957 in Vancouver, Canada, McCarthy received his degrees in Urban Geography and Architecture from the University of British Columbia. He is the founder and chairman of Mosaic Homes, a "design-build" property development company located in Vancouver.

Felipe Mesa
CASA V, with Giancarlo Mazzanti

Born in 1975 in Medellín, Colombia, Mesa studied architecture at the Pontifical Bolivarian University (Medellín) between 1993 and 1998, and received his Master of Architecture from the Polytechnic University of Catalonia (Barcelona) in 2000. He founded Plan:b Arquitectos in 2000. Fellow Pontifical Bolivarian University graduate Alejandro Bernal Camargo joined the firm as partner in 2005, and their work includes a building for the Colegio Hontanares (Medellín, 2006), the Orchideorama of the Botanical Garden of Medellín (Medellín, Antioquia, 2006), and the Click Clack Hotel (Bogota, 2014).

MO+G
CASA EUCALIPTOS

MO+G was founded in Guadalajara in 2012 by Andrés Mayorga García Rulfo, born in 1988, Leopoldo Orendain Ruiz Escoto, born in 1992, and Diego González Díaz Ochoa, born in 1988, all graduates in architecture from the ITESO (Western Institute of Technology and Higher Education, Guadalajara).

Rozana Montiel
ALBINO ORTEGA HOUSE

Born in 1972 in Mexico City, Montiel earned her BA in Architecture and Urban Planning from the Ibero-American University in 1998, and gained an MA in Architectural Theory and Criticism from the Polytechnic University of Catalonia, Barcelona, in 2000. She founded the firm Rozana Montiel | Estudio de Arquitectura in her birthplace, Mexico City, and specializes in architectural design and artistic re-conceptualizations of space and the public domain. Montiel is member of the Editorial Board of the architectural magazine *Arquine*, and has taught architecture at several universities, including the Ibero-American University.

Max Núñez
CASA GHAT

Born in Santiago in 1976, Núñez received his Masters degree from the Pontifical Catholic University of Chile in 2004 before studying at the Polytechnic University of Milan, Italy, between 1998 and 1999. In 2010 he completed a Masters in Advanced Architectural Design at Columbia University, New York, where he received both the Lowenfish Memorial Prize and the William Ware Prize for Excellence in Design. He founded Max Núñez Arquitectos in 2011.

John Osborne
CASA PÁJARO DE PLATA

Osborne received his Bachelor in Architecture from San José's University of Design in 2000, and then became a project architect at RoTo Architects, Los Angeles, until 2006. He then co-founded Laboratory Sustaining Design, Guanacaste, Costa Rica, and served as its Principal between 2006 and 2009, when he founded OS Arquitectura in Guanacaste and Los Angeles in 2009.

Pezo von Ellrichshausen
CASA NIDA, CASA GUNA

This art and architecture studio was established by Mauricio Pezo and Sofía von Ellrichshausen in 2002. Mauricio Pezo, born in Chile in 1973, completed his Masters in Architecture at the Pontifical Catholic University of Chile in 1998. Sofía von Ellrichshausen, born in Argentina in 1976, received her degree in architecture from the University of Buenos Aires in 2002. Together they curated the Chilean Pavilion at the 2008 Venice Architecture Biennale.

PRODUCTORA
CASA DIAZ

This firm based in Mexico City was founded in 2006 by Abel Perles, born in Argentina in 1972, Carlos Bedoya, born in 1973 in Mexico, Victor Jaime, born in 1978 in Mexico, and Wonne Ickx, born in 1974 in Belgium. The name PRODUCTORA, which is Spanish for producer or production company, was chosen in reference to their method of continuous production in testing their designs. Their work has been recognized by the Architectural League of New York's Young Architects Forum and Emerging Voices awards, in 2007 and 2013 respectively.

Smiljan Radic
CASA PAREADAS

Born in 1965 in Santiago, Radic studied architecture at the Pontifical Catholic University of Chile, graduating in 1989, and established his own office in 1995. His work, including the Serpentine Gallery Pavilion in London (2014), has received international acclaim.

Sérgio Sampaio
MARIA & JOSÉ HOUSE

Born in São Paulo in 1975, Sampaio graduated in Architecture and Urbanism from the Mackenzie Presbyterian University in São Paulo in 1998, and postgraduate studies from the city's Escola da Cidade college in 2009. He founded Sérgio Sampaio Arquitetura + Planejamento in 1998, an office that specializes in urban planning, in both private and public sectors.

Manolo F. Ufer
ECOSCOPIC HOUSE

Born in Madrid in 1976, Ufer studied architecture in the United Kingdom, at the University of Edinburgh and at the Architectural Association in London, graduating in 2002. He went on to gain an MSc in Architecture and Urban Design from the Columbia University Graduate School of Architecture Planning & Preservation in New York. He created his own office, archipelagos, in 2007, an architecture studio that specializes in experimental housing.

Cristián Undurraga
CASAS DEL HORIZONTE

Born in Santiago in 1954, Undurraga received his architecture degree from the Pontifical Catholic University of Chile in 1977. In the same year, he obtained the First Prize for Young Architects at the Chilean Architectural Biennale, and in 1978 he created Undurraga Devés Arquitectos. In 2009 he was made an Honorary Fellow of the American Institute of Architects.

Luis Velasco Roldan + Ángel Hevia Antuña
SUSTAINABLE HOUSE

Luis Velasco Roldan received his PhD from the Barcelona School of Architecture in 2006. Since then he has held numerous academic and teaching positions and between 2013 and 2016 was an environmental researcher at the Escuela Politécnica del Ejército, Quito, Ecuador, in the Department of Mechanical Engineering and Energy's Research Group on Renewable Energies. He was nominated to represent Ecuador in the Latin-American Architecture Biennale in 2017. Mallorca-based architect Ángel Hevia Antuña is associated with the Official College of Architects of the Balearic Islands.

WAY
MOINHO VILLA

This studio was established in 2011 by Carlo Costa, born in Milan, Italy, in 1974, and Priscilla Pinotti, born in Campinas, Brazil, in 1977. Carlo Costa studied at the University of the Basque Country, Spain, and the Polytechnic University of Milan, Italy, where he graduated in 2002. He has been involved in projects across the world, including a 62-floor Shangri-La Hotel Tower in Manhattan (New York) and the Canary Wharf Crossrail train station (London). Priscilla Pinotti studied at the Technical University of Madrid, Spain, graduating in 2001, and has worked on the new National Arena for Glasgow, a 12,000-seater multi-function venue.

Isay Weinfeld
CASA YUCATAN, CASA DECK
Born in 1952 in São Paulo, Weinfeld graduated from the
Mackenzie Presbyterian University in São Paulo in 1975.
Weinfeld has also worked in cinema since 1974, making
short films that have received numerous international
awards. In 1988, he co-wrote and co-directed his first
full-length movie (with Marcio Kogan), *Fogo e Paixão*.
Weinfeld has completed dozens of private homes,
commercial projects, banks, advertising agencies,
discotheques, bars, restaurants, an art gallery, and the
Hotel Fasano (São Paulo, 2001–3, with Marcio Kogan).
He is currently working on the new location of the
Four Seasons Restaurant in New York.

WMR
CABANAS PURA VIDA
The Santiago-based studio WMR was founded in 2005,
taking its name from the partners' surnames—Wedeles,
Manieu, Rabat—all of whom studied at the Finis Terrae
University in Santiago. Felipe Wedeles Tondreau was born
in 1977, and obtained his architectural degree at the Finis
Terrac University in 2001. Jorge Manieu Briceno was born
in 1976, obtaining his degree in architecture in 1999.
He worked with Felipe Assadi prior to co-founding WMR.
Macarena Rabat Errazuriz was born in 1982, and previously
worked at ZS Architects.

Cazú Zegers
CASA GRANERO
Born in Santiago in 1958, Zegers graduated in architecture
from the Pontifical Catholic University of Chile in 1984.
Since 1990 she has worked on architectural projects, urban
planning, and cultural and territorial management, as well
as lamp and furniture design. Her industrial design work,
interior architecture, and residential buildings follow
a low-technology approach: Her Tierra Patagonia Hotel
(Torres del Paine, Chile, 2011) demonstrates her capacity
to take wooden architecture, in this case in the shape of
an "old fossil, a prehistoric animal beached on the shore
of the lake, not unlike those found and studied by Charles
Darwin," to a much larger scale with success.

PICTURE CREDITS

On the cover: Casa Cubo © Fernando Guerra / VIEW

First published in the United Kingdom in 2018 by Thames & Hudson Ltd,
181A High Holborn, London WC1V 7QX

Casa Moderna: Latin American Living © 2018 Thames & Hudson Ltd, London

Designed by Peter Dawson, gradedesign.com

British Library Cataloguing-in-Publication Data
A catalogue record for this book is available from the British Library

ISBN 978-0-500-34329-6

Printed and bound in China by Imago Publishing Limited

To find out about all our publications, please visit **www.thamesandhudson.com**.
There you can subscribe to our e-newsletter, browse or download our current catalogue,
and buy any titles that are in print.